D1116411

Introductions in Feminist Theology

12

Editorial Committee

Mary Grey
Lisa Isherwood
Janet Wootton

Other titles in the series:

Rosemary Ruether, *Introducing Redemption in Christian Feminism*
Lisa Isherwood and Elizabeth Stuart, *Introducing Body Theology*
Melissa Raphael, *Introducing Thealogy: Discourse on the Goddess*
Pui-lan Kwok, *Introducing Asian Feminist Theology*
Janet H. Wootton, *Introducing a Practical Feminist Theology of Worship*
Mary Grey, *Introducing Feminist Images of God*
Mercy Amba Oduyoye, *Introducing African Women's Theology*
Lisa Isherwood, *Introducing Feminist Christologies*
Musimbi R.A. Kanyoro, *Introducing Feminist Cultural Hermeneutics*
Natalie K. Watson, *Introducing Feminist Ecclesiology*
Zoë Bennett Moore, *Introducing Feminist Perspectives on Pastoral Theology*

Nyack College Library

HQ
1061
'E22
2005

Introducing Ecofeminist
Theologies

Heather Eaton

T & T CLARK INTERNATIONAL
A Continuum imprint
LONDON • NEW YORK

Published by T&T Clark International
A Continuum imprint
The Tower Building, 11 York Road, London SE1 7NX
15 East 26th Street, Suite 1703, New York, NY 10010

www.tandtclark.com

All rights reserved. No part of this publication may be reproduced or transmitted in any form or by any means, electronic or mechanical, including photocopying, recording or any information storage or retrieval system, without permission in writing from the publishers.

Copyright © Heather Eaton, 2005

British Library Cataloguing-in-Publication Data
A catalogue record for this book is available from the British Library

Typeset by ISB Typesetting, Sheffield
Printed on acid-free paper in Great Britain by Hobbs the Printers, Hampshire

#5742947S

ISBN 0-567-08207-5 (paperback)

Table of Contents

Editor's Preface

Ecofeminism, it has been said, is a new word for an old wisdom. Linking the age-old oppression of women and earth, it represents a new stage in ecological thinking. It also represents a new stage in Liberation Theology itself. As Leonardo Boff expressed it in the subtitle of his book, *Ecology and Liberation: A New Paradigm*. [1] 'New' it may be in the consciousness of Liberation Theology and ecological theory, but for those communities of women struggling for water, food and animal fodder – the resources that sustain life itself – not much has changed over the centuries. But at last the urgency of the ecological crisis has highlighted these issues, and public consciousness has begun to make the connections.

This book, eagerly awaited, is a vital contribution to the *Introductions in Feminist Theology* series, a series appreciated by students, teachers and practitioners alike. Heather Eaton, Professor of ecological theology in Ottawa, has long been recognized as a significant figure in the field of ecological theology and ecofeminism in Canada and the United States. Through this book – that displays her command of the field of ecofeminism – her work will become widely known and used also on this side of the water.

The skill that she manifestly displays here is to weave together the many disciplines and voices that form ecofeminist theology – history, philosophy, anthropology and science being important dialogue partners. So, whereas there are many books on various aspects of ecofeminism, this book's strength and uniqueness is to bring all this diversity into creative interplay as authentic theology. Whereas she makes it clear that ecofeminist theology can never be a formal systematic theology in the traditional sense, precisely because of its numerous formative currents and strands – she uses the flexible metaphor of the intersections of roads and pathways to describe these – Heather Eaton writes with clarity, poetic fervour, imagination and conviction. What holds the discipline together is the logic of domination – with ruthless consequences for women and earth alike – and this is traced in its philosophical dimension, in the part it played in the rise of patriarchy and in its current manifestations in religion and culture. Although the Christian faith is the main dialogue partner, the book also engages with many faiths and with goddess traditions, and gives poignant examples of the difference ecofeminist practice can make in the achievement of justice.

I have high hopes that this will be a book that makes a difference and believe it will be widely read, appreciated and acted upon.

Mary Grey, July 2004

Acknowledgements

This book, *Introducing Ecofeminist Theologies,* began with an invitation from Anne Primavesi to collaborate on co-writing it for the series. While Anne moved on to more scientific pastures, her inspiration remained. A special thanks to Mary Grey and Lisa Isherwood for their patience. To those who read parts of this manuscript en route, Sam Shortt, Eileen Kerwin Jones, Jessica Fraser and Mary Grey, a further thanks. To incredible teachers, communities of friends, scholars, and activists who have challenged and supported me, and with whom I have worked for many years attempting to understand better why we need to address the ecological crisis together with gender, you are the best! In gratitude for my family, Amelia and Doug, for all that they do to make life good, and work possible. And with immense gratitude to the earth for this one wild and precious life!

Heather Eaton

Introduction

Since the roots of our ecological troubles are so largely religious, the remedy must also be essentially religious. We must rethink and refeel our nature and destiny. Lynn White, Jr (1967: 1207).

And God said let there be life, and life in abundance. And let it fill the earth (Genesis 1).

Currently twenty-five per cent of all mammals are threatened with extinction. All large mammals will be extinct in Africa in twenty years if they are not deliberately protected, from habitat loss or degradation, and hunting. Thirty to fifty per cent of all fish are threatened, as is one in three plants.

Over hundreds of millions of years, Earth developed a stable climate. Volcanoes expelled hot magma to the surface and steam condensed above the Earth; the miracle of rain and weather cycles began. The first rains fell, and for three hundred million years it rained on earth – day and night – cooling the earth, developing a stable climate structure: a staggering feat of ingenuity and brilliance.

Climate change will result in disruptions of food supplies, polluted water resources and human disease. Reading deeper into the signs of weather disruptions, it is evident that climate change disproportionally affects those in the South, and in particular those in coastal areas. They are also the most poor and vulnerable, and with the least resources to mitigate the damage or affect of change.

Water is ever moving in a delicately balanced and infinitely sophisticated system. Water evaporates from the oceans, rises into the earth's atmosphere and falls back on earth as fresh water – such stunning gracefulness and elegance of the earth's system.

Water, the source of life; Living water; Still waters run deep; You will become a fountain of living water; water like a mighty river; longing for running water.

'...water water everywhere, but not a drop to drink.' The World Health Organization, the United Nations, and the World Bank know that within twenty years over two-thirds of the world's people will experience severe potable water shortages. This does not include animals and plants.

In six months of breast-feeding, a baby in Europe or North America gets the maximum lifetime recommended dose of dioxin and five times the allowable daily level of PCBs set by international standards for a 150 pound adult.

There are currently over twenty million environmental refugees in the world, much higher than political refugees. Between seventy-five and ninety per cent of all refugees are women and children.

Humans cannot bear much reality (T.S. Eliot, from Burnt Norton).

To violate the earth is to tear God's masks, to scar God's physical face, to desecrate God's earthly dwelling (Normal Habel).

I said to the tree, speak to me of God, and it blossomed (Sufi).

Tell me, what is it you plan to do with your one wild and precious life? (Mary Oliver).

Introduction

To be alive today is to experience immense political, social and ecological changes. It is difficult to imagine more serious challenges than those the human communities face today. Of the many responses to these challenges, the joining of the ecological and feminist movements provides a way to perceive, under-stand, and transform some of these difficult realities. Ecological-feminism, or ecofeminism, represents an influential collaboration and potent transformative potential.

This book is about ecofeminism and its encounter with theology, pre-dominantly that of Christian theology in Euro-western contexts. It introduces ecofeminism, and explores this encounter. One goal is to understand the sig-nificance and implications of ecofeminism and its contribution and challenge to theology. A further goal is to support ecofeminist theology, or theologies, to be more effective in preventing ecological ruin, in assisting women's struggles for freedom and in sustaining the flourishing of all life on earth.

What is Ecofeminism? Chapter One

Ecofeminism is about connections between ecological and feminist concerns. It is a way of discerning associations of many kinds between the feminist and ecological movements, and between the oppression and domination of women and the oppression and domination of the earth. Ecofeminism is an insight, an exposition of current problems, and an eco-political strategy. It refers to critical analyses, political actions, historical research, intuitions and ideals. Ecofeminism is a term that now shelters hosts of different links between feminism and ecology, and between women and the natural world. It is an evolving phenomena created by the convergence of two important contemporary movements – ecology and feminism. For many, ecofeminism represents the third wave of feminism.[1]

The term 'ecofeminism' was coined by French feminist Françoise d'Eaubonne in *Le Féminisme ou la Mort* (1974) when she called upon women to lead an ecological revolution to save the planet. Today what is included within the term 'ecofeminism' is comparable to an intersection of many roadways. It is like a hub, or roundabout, where one meets academics and activists, environmentalists and feminists, religious and non-religious types, and local and international groups. It represents a large range of analyses and actions including historical associations between women and nature, studies of and resistance to domination as a mode of inter-human and human–earth relations, in depth understanding of patriarchal social structures and worldviews, and, social movements that see the oppression of women and the domination of the natural world as interconnected. Militarism, biotechnology, economic globalization, and privatization of earth resources are only a few of the items looked at by ecofeminists. These are studied in terms of their ecological impact as well as

---

1. The notion of women's equality has existed for centuries. The term 'feminism' was coined in 1895. An organized or first wave feminism did not appear until the late 1700s in Britain and the early 1800s in America. First wave feminism refers to a middle class women's movement working for the reform in social and legal inequalities. Mary Wollstonecraft's *A Vindication of the Rights of Woman* (1792), was the first published in-depth look at women in British society. In the United States the women's suffrage movement emerged from the temperance and anti-slavery causes. In 1848 Elizabeth Cady Stanton and Lucretia Mott organized the famous Seneca Falls Convention where they declared '…all men and women are created equal.' These examples, and the audacious efforts for women to be able to vote, are part of first wave feminism. Second wave feminism refers to the re-emergence of feminist activity in the 1960's in Europe, Britain and North America. It was predominantly an activist movement joining with anti-war, anti-nuclear, environment, and anti-racism.

Ynestra King, one of the founders of US ecofeminism, considers that ecofeminism, the most recent manifestation of feminist activity, is parallel in size and vitality to the other two surges of the women's movement. Mentioned in Noël Sturgeon, *Ecofeminism Natures: Race, Gender, Feminist Theory and Political Action* (New York: Routledge, 1997): 24,200. Ecofeminist theorists Karen Warren and Val Plumwood find ecofeminism represents a third wave of feminist ventures. See Warren, 'Feminism and Ecology: Making Connections', *Environmental Ethics* 9(1): 3-20; Plumwood, 'Feminism and the Mastery of Nature' (New York: Routledge, 1993): 39.

their correlation to issues of ethnicity, class, and gender. Ecofeminists see social and ecological justice and peace are to be inextricably linked.

Ecofeminism has proven to be an enormously useful and flexible insight. The image I use throughout the book is that of a busy traffic roundabout with many roads coming in and going out. As such, it is a broad understanding that I seek, in order to include many voices and perspectives. Chapter One introduces these above aspects of ecofeminism, and gives an overview of its meanings, developments, and analyses.

Women and the Natural World: Chapter Two
A focal insight of ecofeminism is that historical, symbolic, political and economic relationships exist between the denigration of the natural world and the oppression of women in Euro-western cultures. This has been especially true over the last one thousand years. Ecofeminists make a historical claim that women and the natural world have been interrelated; that is, that women were considered to be close to nature, and nature was deemed to be feminine. These became associated together, and both were considered inferior. I refer to this as the women/nature nexus. They were connected to ways of perceiving the world in opposites or dualisms, such as heaven/earth, culture/nature, men/ women, and spirit/matter. An understanding of the historical claim, and the dualisms and their impact, are part of Chapter Two.

The 'nature' of women is a central theme in patriarchal societies. Patriarchy has been the dominant worldview for several thousand years. Although feminism has cracked parts of patriarchy, this long legacy of patriarchy remains the cultural foundation and is our heritage. It has become part of the cultural-symbolic worldview. Ecofeminism seeks to understand in depth this heritage, analyse how it functions, and denounce its limitations. The second chapter delves into the quest for origins to understand how the domination of women and the destruction of the natural world may have come about, so as to grapple with these dominations today. It will also consider the limits as well as the strengths of the ecofeminist claims.

The Ecological Crisis and Religion: Ecofeminism and Theology: Chapter Three
The annual *State of the World* report leaves no doubt that we are in an ecological crisis, that all levels of ecological health are affected, and that the outcomes are unpredictable. Conferences abound on how to understand and what to do about climate change, extreme species extinction, billions of tons of top soil loss, and ozone depletion. Water is becoming a critical issue. The aquifers are shrinking and becoming toxic. In most Euro-western water systems, levels of

oestrogen-like compounds from organic chlorides are so high that many inhabitants of the waterways are unable to reproduce because their reproductive organs have mutated. And on it goes. The effects on human health are already being felt, and globally. The effects on earth health and integrity of complex life-systems are virtually unknown. For the majority, the litany of ecological horrors is overwhelming, and we feel we have few resources to authentically respond to the magnitude of the crisis. Equally, the big players in ecological ruin – the banks, businesses, corporations, the international economic system, and the militaries – seem far removed from the daily life of many citizens and religious leaders.

Chapter Three presents briefly the problems between the ecological crisis and Christianity. It then describes how ecotheologians and ecofeminists are responding. Ecofeminist perspectives are seeping into all aspects of religious understanding. The slow but steady accumulation of work bringing ecofeminist analyses to bear on religious histories, systematic theologies, scriptural interpretations, spiritualities and ethics is creating, not only unique resources but formidable challenges. Some ecofeminists are studying and exposing the negative histories and practices of their traditions. Others are sifting through texts and teachings for insights, redeeming what is helpful and negating what is not. Ecofeminists probe religious traditions for their part in developing and sustaining anti-women and anti-earth worldviews. Other work involves the reinterpretation, expansion or creation of particular doctrines, symbols and metaphors that include and honour women and the natural world. Those engaging ecofeminism with religious and spiritual traditions, while finding valuable resources, also show that there are limitations. Much of the chapter looks at the differences between examining distinct parts of theology, such as doctrines or biblical texts, and examining the whole of theology and the very way theology is done.

Ecofeminist Earth-Centred and Liberation Theologies: Chapter Four
The ecological crisis is provoking a profound cultural revisioning, and new ways of thinking. This process is calling forth a theological renewal and is creating a new context for theology. A religious sensitivity towards the earth is emerging and requires theological attention, spurred on by novel insights in science and spirituality. The awareness of the integrity of the earth, the religious influence on cultural practices towards the natural world, and the global/local nature of many communities are shifting inter-religious collaboration into a more comprehensive realm. The basic assumptions of religious 'truths' and traditions are being shaped in this new global ecological context.

Chapter Four looks at the two particular forms of ecofeminist theologies. As a result of gleaning knowledge from the earth sciences (evolutionary biology, ecosystems science, cosmology), some ecofeminist theologians sense the extent of the challenge facing humanity in general and religious reflection in particular. Humans need to be understood as one species among many, within a complex and magnificent unfolding of the universe and life on earth. Knowing the earth as part of a living universe broadens our consciousness and creates possibilities of new ways of knowing the earth, and in consequence, resisting its destruction. These earth-centred or cosmological ecofeminist efforts are the first topic of chapter four.

The second topic is that resistance to and elimination of oppression are central intents of ecofeminism. Increasingly, ecofeminist theology is connecting with liberation theories and theologies. A passionate concern for justice animates a growing aspect of ecofeminist theological contributions that I am referring to as ecofeminist liberation theologies. Ecofeminist liberationist perspectives move beyond education into active political engagement.

Examples of both of these ecofeminist theologies will be discussed throughout Chapter Four. The goal is to unite the earth-centred and liberation ecofeminist theologies. Ecological-feminist theologies need to establish a vision of a divine or sacred presence that is both embedded in and sustains natural earth processes and also grapples with the social, political and economic forces that create victims of many members of the earth community.

Gathering Forces: Chapter Five
Chapter Five gathers the hermeneutics or guiding principles that have been developing at the intersection of ecofeminism and theology and discussed throughout the book. Each is presented in terms of the insights it offers, and how it needs to be advanced so that religious efforts in ecofeminism will be more compelling, nuanced and transformative. The goal is to understand the contributions, as well as to plot out some future directions for ecofeminist theologies.

A Few Definitions
There are multiple roadways in and out of the ecofeminist intersection, and each has particular sets of concerns, analyses and definitions. At times each route has its own signposts and terminology. Overall, however, ecofeminists assume that some concepts are readily understood, when they may not be. A few of these are the following. **Misogyny** refers to a fear, disrespect, hatred and/or distrust of women. **Anthropocentrism** means a human-centred framework, and one that assumes human supremacy. **Androcentrism** refers

to a male-centred framework. Other more general but often used words are **radical**, meaning at the root of things. **Empirical** or material reality refers to the concrete way life is lived. This includes the economic mode of existence, the facts and figures about social organization. This empirical analysis may or may not be in sync with our ideas about the world. Ideas and ideals about the world and how it should be are called the cultural-symbolic level, and are embedded in our worldviews. These are often hidden from our everyday awareness. **Worldview** means the overall belief system about the world, the values out of which we live, our role in the scheme of things, what is considered to be good, moral and immoral, and basically how things ought to be. A **logic of domination** is an often-used termed coined by ecofeminist philosopher Karen Warren, and it refers to the combined patterns of domination that make up Euro-western societies, such as those based on ethnicity, class, gender, sexual orientation and the natural world (Warren 1990: 133). The most difficult word to use is **God**. When I use the word God I am referring to a cluster of images. For example, God is… a verb, a presence, a power, an energy, and an ethic. God is like the wind, or as the passage of Ezekiel describes that God is not in the earthquake, or the fire or the storm, but God is within the whispering wind, or as in another translation, the thundering silence. God is a metaphoric and symbolic referent for the ineffable dimension of existence, that which is Divine and Sacred, and within what is experienced as divine and sacred. The image 'God' is only one of endless possibilities: Goddess, Mystery, Spirit, Sacred, Holy or other metaphors. Each is a distinct metaphor referring to particular experiences. Many religions' traditions are non-theistic. They attend to the world of religious experiences with images, rituals and language that evoke awareness or contemplation such as Buddhism, or to tune into the patterns of life embedded within earth and human processes, such as the Dao.

A Few Comments

Ecofeminism is an insight and a practice. However ecofeminism is really ecofeminisms. It is used by many diverse groups of women, in multiple contexts and in a huge variety of ways. It is helpful to remember that there has never been an idea or intellectual position that does not appear in many forms and has not changed through history. Ecofeminism is like a busy traffic roundabout that is continually in motion. Although books and courses about ecofeminism try to find boundaries and concepts, the reality always spills over.

Much of the religious ecofeminist work is in reinterpretations of Christianity, within many Christian denominations although often within Catholic traditions, and usually in English. There are several possible reasons for this. One is that much of early feminist religious reflections have emerged from Christian or post-Christian women. A second is that many feminist/religious publications occur in English speaking regions of the world. A third may be due to the historically aggressive thrust of Christianity and its hegemonic influences. A fourth may be that for decades Christianity has been scrutinized in universities, and at times can be reworked without extreme official opposition. A fifth is that feminism has been able to find a social/political space in some cultures more readily than others, and that the international feminist conversation is predominantly in English. Regardless, the fact remains that much of the ecofeminist religious work is Christian, or largely influenced by Christianity, and in English. This book emerges out of these contributions. It is not intended to represent other than Euro-western cultural analyses, and even then only in a limited way.

More importantly, we need to realize that the basic context of the intersection of women, religion and ecology is really lived close to the ground and around the world. Here, in the daily and unremitting survival requirements, women from distinct religious traditions often collaborate to make life manageable and desirable. Here is where we unite together for clean water for children in schools, for non-toxic food, and for an end to violence. It is on the land that women eke out a barely subsistence living for their families and themselves, and pray for change. It is here that our spiritualities are woven into the fabric of our lives and land, consciously or not, within coherent theoretical frameworks, or not. It is the daily struggles that compel us to bring our friends and neighbours from numerous cultural and religious backgrounds out to events, protests, meetings, and social fora. And here, in the market place of the world, we meet, live with, and try to co-operate with others with whom we share some, but not all, of our distinctiveness. It is in this place, close to the ground, where commitments and convictions are navigated, that the bulk of the intersection of women, religion and ecology is lived out. It is difficult to know and tell these stories, and impossible to bring them into conceptual orderliness for a book about ecofeminism and religion. Such discussions, even in this book, are a truncated version of the intricate, daily, convoluted, contradictory and muddled interactions of real living, of our changing spiritual insights and of the things we do to sustain life and to try to change the world. It simply must be remembered that in the following theoretical discussion about ecofeminism and religion, and in the translating of activism into print, much of the 'real world' is lost in the translation.

A Few Convictions

The ecological crisis is accepted here as the most serious quandary of this, and perhaps any, human epoch. A viable future depends upon decisions made by the current generation. The present period of mass extinction is comparable to those 65, 94, 213 and 248 million years ago (Livingston 1994: 1). Then we add in climate change, pollution, biotechnology, soil erosions and deforestation, and their contributions to human cancers, asthma, flu epidemics, and viruses, and we can begin to see the magnitude of the ecological crisis. These are only the effects on human animals. Other forms of life are suffering immensely. Also, social and ecological crises are often interlocked and one cannot be resolved without the other. The United Nations predicts that in twenty years two-thirds of all people will have limited access to water. What about water for plants or animals?

The ecological crisis is not an addendum to the increasing numbers of social ills. There is no question that future generations of humans will live in a wholly different world, with fewer trees, poor air quality, unstable climates, a lack of water, diminished biodiversity, sparse arable land, few large animals and increased illnesses. These are direct consequences of a disregard of the earth. Thomas Berry writes: 'Future generations will live not only amid the ruined infrastructures of the industrial world but also amid the ruins of the natural world itself' (Berry 1986: 1). Children everywhere in the world are growing accustomed to not drinking from rivers and lakes, or swimming in them, of having respiratory problems from air pollution, and assuming ecological problems are the given reality. It is necessary to avoid a gradual and perhaps unconscious sinking into a dispassionate acceptance of the diminishing of earth's health.

The ecological crisis is creating a pivotal moral and religious challenge, indeed a new context or contexts for theology. In the midst of this turmoil, and within the realm of spirituality, (considered to be prior to and foundational for theology), there is a renewed spiritual sensitivity towards the natural world. Perhaps due to the accelerating devastation of the earth there is a renewed interest in the association between spirituality and ecological well-being. We are in a time of a spiritual awakening, wherein the earth and all life are experienced, once again, as sacred. Such a religious or spiritual sensitivity is both a primeval and a contemporary awareness.

We are in a new revelatory moment where classical religious experiences are happening. It is a new and very old dance. Once again it is possible to be enveloped by awe and wonder, and to encounter the ineffable. Awe and wonder are powerful, and they cannot be tamed. Neither can the earth nor the Divine be tamed, in spite of all our efforts to domesticate, dominate, reduce and name them, or make them manageable as to fit our conceptual structures. Humans are simply not the reference point of the earth and the universe.

Ecofeminist theologies are at the intersection of these concerns, ideas and experiences. They represent the efforts of particular people who see and experience possibilities for greater life, more justice and freedom. They do not accept that injustice and ecological ruin are inevitable. They create the potential to change the world. For these efforts, and those still to come, I am grateful. All these ecofeminist efforts are directed towards reducing further ecological and social devastation. Ecofeminism is one offering that may awaken our consciousness to the immense beauty and elegance of all life on this fragile yet awesome blue-green planet.

Chapter One

Ecological-feminism: Overview and Development

Ecofeminism: A Definition

Ecofeminism came on to the cultural scene in North America and Europe in the early 1970s. It was an appealing and inspiring connection that quickly made sense to people already working for social change. Ecofeminism, broadly presented, is a convergence of the ecological and feminist analyses and movements. It represents varieties of theoretical, practical and critical efforts to understand and resist the interrelated dominations of women and nature. Ecofeminism, like ecology and feminism, is heterogeneous and has distinguishable components. While ecofeminists share a basic awareness of connections between women and the natural world, there are different entry points and distinct sets of concerns, orientations and political goals. Ecofeminism stands for a diversity of approaches and perspectives. Most of ecofeminism comes from and speaks to Euro-western cultures, although not exclusively. It is however global in scope, meaning that global issues and links are crucial to ecofeminist theories and actions. Ecofeminism wraps many items in its package (Prentice 1988: 9).

Given that ecofeminism covers a large range of activities, and represents many ideals and ideas, a useful image is that of a busy roundabout intersection. There are many pathways in and out of the intersection, and lots of traffic! Some paths are well travelled and others less so.

The development of ecofeminism is fascinating. How, in twenty years, has this term 'ecofeminism' been picked up and used in such diverse ways? How has it attained many meanings? How does such an insight make its way into a culture? How does it become a useful analysis? Somehow ecofeminism caught the cultural imagination of enough people in the feminist and ecological movements.

A Busy Intersection

There are many ways to bring together ecology and feminism, and I am taking a broad and inclusive definition of ecofeminism. Although differences are important at times, I am including all types of ecological-feminist connections. I am not distinguishing between those who identify as ecofeminists and those who connect feminism with ecology or women with environmental issues but do not use the term 'ecofeminism'. For present purposes, an encompassing understanding allows for the wide spectrum of analyses, critiques and activities that enter the busy, at times congested, ecofeminist intersection.

Finding a way to present ecofeminism is challenging! It is an image, a connection and an analysis that is very recent. It emerged organically in different parts of the world. Yet, to understand ecofeminism is to appreciate the particular origins out of which it came, which are predominantly Euro-western. The following conversation is divided into three sections: history and development, contributions and congestion, and commentary. Together these shed some light on the progressive expansion of ecofeminism, and what have surfaced as the main issues.

Ecofeminism: History and Development

Ecofeminism is akin to an intersection point of multiple pathways. People came to ecofeminism from many directions, and have taken it to other places, disciplines and actions. It is impossible to provide a straightforward narrative of the origins and evolution of ecofeminism, as its development is neither straightforward, nor does a singular narrative suffice. The following is an attempt to present some of the pathways to ecofeminism, and the women who bring their knowledge, viewpoints and commitments into and out of the ecofeminist hub. Each person and contribution represents myriad other women, groups and social actions. The entry points into the ecofeminism intersection are separated into four pathways: activism and social movements, academia, religion, and global ecofeminism. Each will be described chronologically and independently although they occurred simultaneously and there are crossovers.

Activism, Social Movements and Conferences

Ecofeminism has early roots in a host of activist efforts and movements in North America and Europe. Women came to ecofeminism from a rise of social consciousness characteristic of the 1960's that claimed equity, peace, democracy and ecological integrity. Noël Sturgeon, academic and activist, has carefully documented the many roots of ecofeminism within activist and political movements in the United States (Sturgeon 1997).

Long before ecofeminism was a popular term, women were active on eco-logical issues. The anti-war, anti-racism, and women's movements of the 1960s and 1970s became increasingly influenced by and allied to environmental move-ments. For example, during the invasion of Vietnam, the United States used Agent Orange to defoliate the Vietnamese landscape. This atrocious activity became merged with the image of raped/despoiled women and napalm burnt/scarred children. This sparked anti-war protests that linked women campaign-ing against militarist technologies, sexual assault and devastating ruin of the natural world. The economics of militarism were exposed for the unlimited budgetary resources for weapons, while proportionally decreasing funding for health, education and social programs. At the same time women were protest-ing the pervasive use of toxic pesticides and herbicides in agriculture, such as DDT. These issues and protests became inter-linked, and seen as a violation of people and earth.

As toxic dumping turned into health problems, women organized to ban pesticides and other contaminants in soil, water and air. In 1978 Lois Gibbs, a young mother and homemaker of upstate New York, became one of the first activists to bring the issue of environmental and health disasters to national and international attention. She identified that toxins were causing sicknesses in children. Her efforts led to the relocation of 833 households of Love Canal, New York. Another example is the Greenham Common Women's Peace Camp. In September 1981 thirty-six women marched for ten days from their south Wales homes to the Berkshire airbase in protest against America's plans to store cruise missiles at the site. The group, called Women for Life on Earth, became the Greenham Common Women's Peace Camp, and as of 1982 the camp became women-only. At times there were 30,000 women at Greenham, and over the years many were arrested and imprisoned. The peace camp and protest lasted eighteen years!

These events began to influence the development of 'green' politics. With the rise of ecological disasters and consciousness, ecological or 'green' political parties formed, particularly in Germany and the United States. Ecofeminism was an aspect of these green political movements, with Petra Kelly inspiring leadership. Connections between women's and environmental issues were brought into the mainstream of a developing political-ecology agenda.

Ecofeminism became an explicit focus in some places. Citizens held rallies and speakers' series, and engaged in numerous consciousness-raising activities. Conferences brought diverse people together and vitalized the activist and con-ceptual connections between women and ecological concerns. Significant gatherings in the United States were *Women and the Environment*, in Berkeley,

California in 1974, and *Women and Life on Earth*, held in Amherst, Massachusetts in 1980. At the latter meeting over 600 women discussed ecological-feminist theory and action, which led to the peace initiative *Women's Pentagon Action* later that year, when 2000 women surrounded the Pentagon. In 1987 the University of Southern California, Los Angeles hosted an event called *Ecofeminist Perspectives*. These conferences united large numbers of people working on a range of issues and brought ecological-feminist associations into public places. Ecofeminism began representing women working in toxic waste, health, media, spirituality, art, theater, energy, urban ecology, or conservation and from the stance of theorist, activist, educator, dreamer or social critic.

Environmental issues were becoming more serious around the world, and it was evident that nations had to address them. The United Nations launched a call to deliberate 'environment and development'. In consultation with a vast array of citizen's groups, experts and national leaders proposed an agenda for sustainable development for the twenty-first century, *Agenda '21*. In 1991, as the world prepared for the 1992 *United Nations Conference on Environment and Development* (UNCED) in Rio de Janeiro, women came from around the world to discuss and present an alternative and progressive feminist and ecological agenda. Women, especially from Southern countries, gathered at the *World Women's Congress for a Healthy Planet,* Miami Florida and produced the *Women's Action Agenda '21*.[1] Although the preparations for UNCED and the proposed *Agenda '21* were intended to include a variety of viewpoints, there was a blatant disregard for the relationship between women, ecology and development. *Women's Action Agenda '21* is a document about women and the ecological crisis, and became a significant catalyst for the connections between women and ecological issues. The document is not simply a litany of horrors, nor idealistic and full of prescriptive promises, but one that makes agency clear. It focuses on a critique of the forces underpinning the problems and offers solutions. The preamble is candid about the intent and analysis. Excerpts include:

> We speak on behalf of the women who experience daily the violence of environmental degradation…
> We are outraged by the inequities…

> As long as 'Nature' and women are abused by a so-called freemarket ideology and wrong concepts of economic growth, there can be no environmental security…

> We will no longer tolerate the enormous role played by the military establishments…

---

1.   http://www.earthsummit2002.org/toolkits/Women/ngo_doku/ngo_conf/ngoearth women1.htm or http://www.iisd.org/women/action21.htm (8 December 2003).

We pledge our commitment to the empowerment of women, the central and powerful force in the search for equity.

We demand our right, as half the world's population, to bring our perspectives, values, skills, and experiences into policy-making...

We equate lack of political and individual will among world leaders with a lack of basic morality and spiritual values and an absence of responsibility towards future generations.

The text covers a wide range of related topics, and is divided into sections that give concrete evidence of the problems, as well as reactions, concerns, and actions that will be taken. Within each section the gender-nature association is obvious. The sections of the *Women's Action Agenda '21* are as follows:

- Democratic Rights, Diversity, and Solidarity
- Code of Environmental Ethics and Accountability
- Women, Militarism, and the Environment
- Debt and Trade
- Women, Poverty, Land Rights, Food Security, and Credit
- Women's Rights, Population Policies, and Health
- Biotechnology and Biodiversity
- Nuclear Power and Alternative Energy
- Science and Technology Transfer
- Women's Consumer Power
- Information and Education

Each section includes between six and ten commitments to actions, and there are eighty-nine such pledges in the document. The report indicates that thorough research, analysis and critique were carried out prior to its completion. The *Women's Action Agenda '21* made numerous recommendations to the United Nations and the donor countries to implement sustainable ecological practices and gender equity. It is a comprehensive and specific account of the gravity and the multifarious nature of the destructive patterns that are devastating to women and the earth, especially in poor countries. As well, it offers precise guidelines and vision to redress some of the central ills that have led to the crisis.

The *Women's Action Agenda '21* is a document primarily of feminist socio-political analysis and plan of action. It represents the first international ecofeminist manifesto. These women were determined to get the limits of the economic system, militarism, agro-business and women's labour on the table. Its strengths are immense. A weakness is that the ecological paradigm is not well developed, meaning ecological ruin is pertinent only when there is human detriment.

During the 1980s and early 1990s ecofeminist vitality and visions were evident. The activist groups, conferences, academics and socially engaged citizens formed a base from which, over time, one could refer to ecofeminism and make sense. It was not a world of ideas and ideals, but a set of connections that congealed over time. Yet ecofeminism was never one reality, vision or practice, and diverse perspectives emerged.

Ecofeminist conversations were appearing in popular publications. The feminist and ecological links were becoming obvious to activists, social theorists and those working on women, environment and development. It became possible to begin to develop ecofeminist theory(ies) and ecofeminist political philosophies. Ecofeminism began to shift from a large set of interconnections to both in-depth historical critiques of the past, and cultural and intellectual analyses of a viable and alternative future for women and the earth. Ecofeminists began to focus their gaze on a cultural-symbolic level of the problems.

Specific publications came into the traffic intersection and were influential in shaping what ecofeminism means. Susan Griffin, author of *Women and Nature: The Roaring Inside Her* (1978) artistically exposed historical evidence of the depth of hostility towards women and the inseparable abhorrence of nature within Christianity, Euro-western science, and philosophy. Mary Daly wrote *Gyn/Ecology: The Metaethics of Radical Feminism* (1978) and not only analysed the historical identification of women with nature but supported women as being different from, and more rooted in nature, than men. In the early 1980s women, such as social ecologist and political activist Ynestra King, then of the Social Ecology Institute in Vermont, developed theoretical connections to promote the holistic and political vision of ecofeminism. Interdisciplinary ecofeminist anthologies appeared, and created larger definitions of what ecofeminism means. Ecofeminist books became popular, such as those by Carolyn Merchant, *The Death of Nature: Women, Ecology and the Scientific Revolution* (1982), Vandana Shiva, *Staying Alive: Women, Ecology and Development* (1988), Mary Mellor, *Breaking The Boundaries: Towards a Feminist Green Socialism* (1992), Val Plumwood, *Feminism and the Mastery of Nature*, (1993), and *Ecofeminism* by Maria Mies and Vandana Shiva (1993). Edited collections brought more voices and perspectives, such as Andree Collard and Joyce Contrucci, *Rape of the Wild: Man's Violence against Animals and the Earth* (1988); Judith Plant, *Healing the Wounds: The Promise of Ecofeminism* (1989); Irene Diamond and Gloria Orenstein, *Reweaving the World: The Emergence of Ecofeminism* (1990); Carol Adams, *Ecofeminism and the Sacred* (1993); and Rosa Braidotti, *et al.*, *Women, the Environment and Sustainable Development* (1994). These books, from Australia, England, India, Germany, Canada and the United States show that a set of concerns and deliberation were coalescing and coming together under the term ecofeminism. Since the

1990's the proliferation of ecofeminist publications in books and journals is beyond description. In most countries of the world there have been ecofeminist conferences, and countless small and large events, political organizations, actions, art and rituals. With publications and conferences increasing, ecofeminism has moved from being a connection between ecology and feminism and a basis of activism and political strategy, to also being a topic pertinent to universities and colleges.

Academia

Because ecofeminism was such an interesting avenue of exploration, it drew reflections from many academic disciplines. People in philosophy, sociology, political science, religion, ethics, economics, and environmental and women's studies shaped the ecofeminist discourses. In academic circles ecofeminism began to be understood in four ways; as the history of women-nature associations, as a lens through which many disciplines (sociology, psychology, technology, etc.) could be refocused, as an alliance within ecological, political and social movements, and, as a way of seeing how women's concerns (poverty, child care, ethnicity, sexual assaults, health, etc.) are related to the beliefs about what is 'natural' or to environmental degradation. As scholars developed their ecofeminist perspectives, university courses on ecofeminism became widespread. The ecofeminist intersection was getting more traffic!

Academics were active in advancing ecofeminist theory, representing mainly the conceptual, symbolic and cultural associations between women and nature. Merchant's book *The Death of Nature* (1980) linked the mechanistic worldview of modern science with the rise of a market-oriented global economy and the resulting exploitation of human and natural resources. She documented the evolution of a double concept of nature as feminine; one as a nurturing mother providing for the needs of 'man' kind, and two as wild and uncontrollable. Both aspects were identified with women, but it was the second, nature as disorder, which became an important image that had a great impact on Euro-western civilizations. This was the beginning of a forceful and systematic thrust of power and control over nature. The change from nourishing to controlling imagery was directly related to the rise in commercialization, which assigned commodity and monetary value to everything, including living beings. Industrialization used new technologies to 'subdue' the earth. This thrust to control a feminine nature, which was extended to women and the natural world, became entrenched and enshrined in philosophy, religious ideas and science.

It was also transported as Europe extended its influence around the world. Maria Mies shows how much of this ideology of control is the basis of the patriarchal, capitalist economic order: the very foundation of western contemporary culture. Mies makes a further connection between the birth of capitalist patriarchy, the slave trade and the destruction of subsistence economies in the colonies, the persecution of women as witches, and the historical emergence of European science and technology, and its mastery over nature (Mies 1986: 77). The scientific revolution gave birth to technological inventions necessary for warfare and conquest, and violence became 'the key word and key method by which the New Man established his domination.' (Mies 1986: 88) Vandana Shiva of India and ecofeminist theologian Ivone Gebara of Brazil found a similar ideology of control deeply embedded within the colonial and development agendas (Shiva 1988; Gebara 1999).

Ecofeminist philosophy provided important conceptual and historical work, principally by Karen J. Warren. Her edited collections, such as *Ecological-Feminism* (1994), *Ecofeminist Philosophies* (1996), *Ecofeminism: Women, Culture, Nature* (1997), and the book she authored, *Ecofeminist Philosophies* (2000) created a conceptual base for the development of ecofeminist ideas and ideals. Academics engaged with historical and theoretical questions of the women-nature and feminist-ecological linkages.

Other academics came to the connections between women and ecology through science. New insights emerging from the science of ecology moved many to reconsider their understanding of the earth. This ranged from an academic study of the complexity and ingenuity of organisms in their environments to a broadly systemic approach to life. The life-sciences were demonstrating the interconnections between the intricate human bodily systems and the systemic nature of the biological systems. They were revealing that in addition to perceiving the distinct spheres of life, there was a functioning of the whole. Whole-systems theories became relevant to understanding science. Evolutionary science revealed that life emerges on earth within infinitely elegant systems of interdependence. This meant that the earth, while infinitely elaborate, also functioned as one global ecosystem, or as a single body.

This insight became important within the ecological movement. The earth was seen as an evolving whole; humans seen as a part of this whole. Some ecofeminists resonated with this unity of the earth. Some saw the earth as the body of God or Goddess, or imbued with divine presence. Others made connections between the treatment of women's bodies and that of the earth. Whether formally articulated or not, the sense of belonging to a system which functions as a whole is an integral part of ecofeminism. It is this sense of belonging within, rather than apart from, nature that propels many ecofeminists.

The intersecting pathways between ecofeminism and science are multiple. Some came through biology, (Rachael Carson, Barbara McKlintock, Evelyn

Fox Keller), where each could sense and reveal scientifically the depth of ingenuity and interdependence of earth systems. Even primatology (Donna Haraway) became a pathway to ecofeminism. Haraway focused on the inter-actions between gender, race and science, and examined the ways in which evolutionary narratives have been given a male bias (Haraway 1993). She discovered that studies of the evolution from primates to humans have been used to support a socio-biological worldview in which competitive, aggressive male traits are taken as determinative of male-female as well as human-nature relationships. Thus competitive, aggressive and dominating male behaviour has been taken to be biologically determined, and therefore justified. Other studies that were less biased would not support these conclusions.

The intersection of women's health and ecological issues was gaining credi-bility. Hazel Henderson is one of several influential doctors who connect human and earth health. Increasingly studies are linking toxins in soils, water contaminants, and even the chlorine in most potable water, to soft tissue cancers in women. The rise of asthma, leukemia and other cancers in children signalled that environmental problems were seeping into the cells of human beings, and having a devastating effect on the most vulnerable. World Health Organization research shows that industrialized countries have far more cancers than countries with little industry. One-half of all the world's cancers occur among people living in industrialized countries, even though such people are only one-fifth of the world's population. Sandra Steingraber's book, *Living Downstream: An Ecologist Looks at Cancer and the Environment* (1997), documents this very carefully. The association between ecological and human health is becoming accepted in mainstream medicine, albeit slowly.

From other academic avenues women were able to converge their expertise and insights at the ecofeminist juncture. Mary Mellor developed a political sociology from an ecofeminist vantage point, connecting economics, politics and a development agenda. Her work, along with ecofeminist political philoso-pher Val Plumwood, feminist economists Marilyn Waring and Bina Agarwal, and numerous other women working at the crossroads of women, poverty, development and environmental ruin has broadened, deepened and politicized ecofeminism. Academics from both science and liberal arts were making eco-feminist connections. These efforts have made ecofeminism relevant outside conceptual and narrow academic venues.

The Road of Religion
While researching the history of the domination of women, which itself is a dreadful and shocking heritage, there is also a legacy of negative women-nature associations that seem constitutive of the religious and philosophical roots of

Euro-western worldviews. The next chapters will discuss these in depth. In short, theological and philosophical analyses of the domination of women within patriarchal social and religious institutional systems showed connections between these and the domination of the natural world. It was becoming clear that women and nature, although at times mutually affirmed, were most often mutually denigrated. Their oppression and liberation were linked together and anchored in both the cultural-symbolic levels and socio-economic relations that sustain patterns of domination.

One of the earliest ecofeminist voices was theologian Rosemary Radford Ruether. In the early 1970s she discerned layers of connections, at least in general terms, among ecology, feminism, and religion. *In New Woman, New Earth* (1975), she called for a prophetic vision to shape a new world on earth, one that was not defined by domination. Out of her passionate concern for justice and a decent life for all, Ruether saw that genuine social justice required a new vision, and perhaps even a new religion. She writes:

> Women must see that there can be no liberation for them and no solution to the ecological crisis within a society whose fundamental model of relationships continues to be one of domination. They must unite the demands of the women's movement with those of the ecological movement to envision a radical reshaping of the basic socio-economic relations and the underlying values of this society. (Ruether 1975: 204)

Women were becoming aware of and outraged by the extensive domination of women. Many were connecting this to struggles they were currently experiencing, such as effective legal action against sexual assault, child support, property ownership, equal pay, and access to all professions. The argument that it was 'natural' for women to live lesser or oppressed lives was rejected outright. The history of the oppression of women became fuel to evaluate and transform present struggles. It was also related to the fact that those most involved in ecological protection were women.

From the mid 1970s to the mid 1980s women from many religious traditions researched women-nature, feminist-ecological questions. Feminist theologians such as Ruether, Ivone Gebara, Anne Primavesi and Mary Grey identified the sources of the domination of women and nature with patriarchal Christianity. Judith Plaskow examined ecofeminism and Judaism. Of several North American Indigenous women addressing ecological concerns, Paula Gunn Allen, a Laguna Pueblo-Sioux, explored practices connecting and ideas about nature, women, spirit and creation. Joanna Macy and Stephanie Kaza gleaned insights from Buddhism to reflect on the ecofeminist challenges. Delores Williams, from a womanist perspective, saw profound connections between the treatment of 'black bodies' and the treatment of women and nature.

In response to both the discovery of the negative history of women and nature, the rise of feminist consciousness and growing ecological concerns, some women became attracted to alternative non-Euro-western, nature-based, and/or ancient Goddess traditions. Historical research revealed evidence of ancient Goddesses, and most pre-dating the patriarchal religions (Eller 2000). Women, including Charlene Spretnak, explored Goddess and earth-based religions, and revived the positive imagery between women and the earth. There emerged an overlap between the earth-centredness of Goddess, Wiccan and Native American spiritualities. Starhawk and thealogian Carol Christ studied how human-nature relations were understood in Goddess, Wiccan and earth-based spiritual traditions. For many of these women, their spiritual orientation was intimately rooted in political activism. For example, Starhawk has brought these insights to bear throughout her campaigns against the Vietnam War, nuclear weapons, and her activities in the pro-democracy and anti-globalization movements.

By the early 1990s ecofeminism was dialoguing with distinct religious traditions. Some of these conversations are found in multi-religious collections, such as one by Rosemary Radford Ruether *Women Healing Earth: Third World Women on Ecology, Feminism and Religion* (1996), *Ecofeminism and the Sacred* (1993) edited by Carol Adams, feminist Buddhist Joanna Macy's *World as Lover, World as Self* (1991), an ecofeminist postmodern spirituality viewpoint in *States of Grace: The Recovery of Meaning in the Postmodern Age* (1991) by Charlene Spretnak, and a multi-religious ecofeminist analysis in Eleanor Rae's *Women, the Earth, the Divine* (1993). These conversations are mostly recorded in publications, which are a limited representation of what is occurring. Still, they offer many teachings, reinterpretations, insights and visions of multiple points of intersections between ecofeminism and religion.

There are also numerous multidisciplinary publications on ecology, and many consider spirituality within the relevant themes. Two early anthologies on ecofeminism, *Healing the Wounds: The Promise of Ecofeminism* (1989) and *Reweaving the World: The Emergence of Ecofeminism* (1990), combine theory and praxis, spirituality and politics, South and North perspectives, and critique and vision. These contributions are indicative of the immense cultural shifts that are occurring. It could be argued that the ecological crisis is causing, perhaps out of necessity, disciplines to collaborate and learn from each other.

Ecological and feminist paths were crossing around the world, and in different religious and cultural traditions. In Chile a group of women founded Con-spirando (a play on words meaning 'breathing with' instead of 'conspiring against'). That for them was a way to communicate an ecological perspective of

bringing together many women to 'breathe with', that is to circulate new energies throughout the earth. The first issue *of Con-spirando: Revista latinoamericana
de ecofeminismo, espiritualidad y teología* was launched on International Women's
Day, 8 March 1992, and has continued into the present (Ress 2003). Many
were making ecological and feminist connections within their traditions and
within their lives.

At this intersection of ecofeminism and religion, some women, as mentioned,
were looking at their religion, while others were addressing issues because of
their religious views. In many instances the religious influence is not obvious.
For example Hindi women were reclaiming land in India, resisting corporate
take-over of agriculture in Latin America, indigenous or Christian women were
contesting patenting of indigenous seeds, opposing dams and deforestation, and
protecting water sources. Theologian Ivone Gebara states that:

> Ecofeminism is born of daily life, of day-to-day sharing among people, of endur-
> ing together garbage in the streets, bad smells, the absence of sewers and safe
> drinking water, poor nutrition and inadequate health care. The ecofeminist issue
> is born of the lack of municipal garbage collection, of the multiplication of rats,
> cockroaches, and mosquitoes, and of the sores on children's skin. This is true
> because it is usually women who have to deal with daily survival issues: keeping
> the house clean and feeding and washing the children. (Gebara 1999: 2)

Women, influenced by religious perspectives, were involved in ecofeminist
projects, although not using the term. Canadian Ursula Franklin, a feminist
physicist and Quaker peace activist, examined the junction between women,
technology and ecological stress. Franklin exposed the attitude of domination
that was concealed within the ideas that technology will bring freedom and
prosperity. She documented the systematic exclusion of women in technology
as well as the resistance to examining the social and ecological consequences of
technology (Franklin 1990). Rosalie Bertell, environmental epidemiologist and
member of the Grey Nuns of the Sacred Heart in the United States, published
her research findings on the relationship between the proximity of nuclear generating stations and increased human illness, such as leukemia (Bertell 1985,
2001). Since the 1970s both women have worked extensively in these areas,
and consistently motivated by justice, feminism, religious views and a concern
for the earth. Women such as they are known as religious activists in addition
to their primary professional work. Others draws from religious insights for
their work, such as Vandana Shiva who reflects on both the Gandhian tradition of nonviolence and the Hindu tradition of the sacredness of the earth in
her work as a feminist scientist. Often it is not possible to assess the role that a
personal spirituality and/or religious conviction plays in motivating individuals.

From another religious vantage point, several feminist-leaning orders of Christian nuns in the United States and Canada are dedicating their vision, mission and property to ecological health and education. This fascinating transformation of Catholic religious sisters is documented in *Green Sisters: Catholic Nuns Answering the Call of the Earth* (McFarland Taylor 2004). Miriam Therese McGillis, Dominican sister and founder of Genesis Farm, is one of these 'green nuns'. She, and others like her, are influencing progressive religious orders to embrace a radical feminist, ecological and political spirituality (Zayac 2003). In the Philippines, the Maryknoll sisters transformed a convent and school at Baguio, Luzon into an ecological educational centre called the Maryknoll Ecological Sanctuary (Rasmussen 2001). Community gardens, health issues, education, public policy, international ecological commitments and toxic dumping are only a few of the concerns of religious sisters. There are dozens of religious orders around the world dedicating themselves to multiple activities at this intersection of religion and ecofeminism.

Religion and Spirituality
It is popular to claim 'I am spiritual but not religious.' Within the religion pathway into ecofeminism there is an aspect of spirituality that at times is connected to religion, and at times is separate. Many women moving out of the confines of patriarchal religious beliefs and spiritual expressions are creating a profusion of 'women's spiritualities'. There is a distinctive women's spirituality movement afoot, reclaiming and rescuing mysticism, cosmology, ritual and faith from patriarchal religions. At times these burgeoning women's spiritualities are ecological. The convictions of peace, ecological integrity, justice, and an awareness of a spiritual dimension to life can form integral elements of ecofeminist spiritualities. Often such a spirituality flourishes where people are perceiving a holistic connection within all life and experiencing a kinship with the earth community.

Within ecofeminist spiritualities are distinct perspectives. While they share a basic connection between women and the earth, like other aspects of ecofeminism their understandings of each and the connections between may differ significantly. Some are essentialist, meaning they connect women to the earth through care, motherhood, menstruation, or an intrinsic feminine psychic and archetypal structure, suggesting that women have more wisdom, knowledge of and desire to protect the earth. For some cultures this is simply accepted as an unquestionable truth. Still, the majority of ecofeminist spirituality is not essentialist. At times the emphasis may be more on transforming women's consciousness than on ecological preservation. There are tremendous insights that the religious voices and developing spiritualities are bringing to the project of ecofeminism and global transformation. The spirituality and religious thought of ecofeminism is rich with wisdom and teachings aimed at amplifying the subtle perceptions of the integrity of life on earth. Many from around the world are joining this search for a living spirituality that honours human life, including women as autonomous agents, and all life within the earth community.

Global Ecofeminism

During the 1980s and 1990s ecofeminism flowered. Women engaged with ecofeminism from various angles, from different parts of the world and within myriad disciplines. Many were intrigued by the term ecofeminism, and what it could mean. Ecofeminism was now an interdisciplinary, multi-focal, and broad-based project, although existing in very small segments of society. At times ecofeminist discussions narrowed to the conceptual and academic venues. At other times it seemed to be 'theoretically' inclusive, yet became detached from the material and economic realities that were shaping daily life for many women and ecosystems. Still at other times ecofeminism was so expansive and sweeping that almost everybody and every concern was included!

As feminism became increasingly global, with much dialogue and debate among women, the relationship between women's issues and ecological concerns grew alongside. By the 1990's sufficient statistics and data on the relationship between ecological stress and several other factors: gender, health, militarism, and economics had accumulated. This became pivotal and challenging to ecofeminism. In 1989 the United Nations reported: 'It is now a universally established fact that it is the woman who is the worst victim of environmental destruction. The poorer she is, the greater is her burden.' (Philiopose 1989: 67) In every country, women make up the majority of the poor (Dankelman and Davidson 1988: 3–5). In most parts of the world environmental problems disproportionately affect women. Data on these harsh realities was emerging, and needed to be integrated into ecofeminist theories, analyses and politics.

The increased burdens women face result not only from environmental deterioration. A sexual division of labour found in most societies considers family sustenance to be women's work. As the primary care givers, women are responsible for the food and health of family members. Due to ecological strain, it is becoming increasingly difficult to provide food, fuel, and water for many families. To make matters worse, many women have little access to economic resources, ownership of land, or commercial businesses. Ecofeminism was exposing a multiplicity of material and economic associations between women and agriculture, land, availability of and access to fuel and water.

Those working at the nexus of gender and development saw the necessity to include an ecological dimension. Core aspects of the 'development' agenda were exposed for their destructive consequences to women and the natural world. Political economist Marilyn Waring demonstrated that the impact of ecological disasters and environmental degradation in poorer countries is greater on women and children than on men, and much greater than on many in industrialized countries (Waring 1988). The life conditions of women and their relationship with ecological realities around the world was becoming known in more places than ever before. The discrepancy between those who have too much and those without enough was extremely obvious. Although ecofeminism appeared to be an advantageous nexus for exchange, some found that the ecofeminist conceptual efforts offered little to women whose livelihood was threatened due to agribusiness, loss of common land, water issues, deforestation and desertification, and enormous levels of poverty and economic powerlessness.

Policies of economic globalization, the World Bank, the International Monetary Fund, and the World Trade Organization were scrutinized and criticized where they created, or demonstrated a lack of concern for, gender and ecological problems. Ecological disasters, like the Exxon oil spill, Bhopal, and Chernobyl, and wars, mega-dams and rainforest destruction, were studied and exposed for their ecological and/or gender wreckage. Women were taking action, such as the Chipko movement in India and the Green Belt forestry reforms in Kenya led by Wangari Mathai.

The global analyses of ethnic oppression and ethnocentrism began to reveal a phenomenon that was termed 'environmental racism'. Toxic dumps were more prevalent in poor Hispanic, Black or indigenous neighbourhoods, or in poverty stricken countries in Africa, Latin America and East Asia. Most often toxic waste is dumped without the knowledge of local peoples, and in areas where citizens have little political power or social cohesion. This spawned a movement for environmental justice, now found in most countries of the world. Ecofeminism connects with environmental justice and adds an analysis of gender.

Ecofeminist policies and practices in one area were supported in another. For example, women protesting the Narmada Dam in India were supported by women in North Atlantic countries. Collaboration between Indian physicist Vandana Shiva, and German social scientist Maria Mies, gave another important focus to global ecofeminism (Shiva and Mies 1993). Their own active involvement in women's and ecological movements in both India and Germany gave them a shared analysis and perspective on the fundamental links between destructive ecological activities, capitalist patriarchal economic systems, colonialization and imposed 'development'. These systems emerged and were built on the colonization of 'foreign' peoples, and by extension on their women, their lands and their natural resources. Mies and Shiva illustrated the bonds between economic globalization, colonization and the appropriation of women and the natural world. The type of postcolonial analysis has been echoed by theologian Ivone Gebara in Brazil, wherein women and their bodies became part of the 'natural resources' to be used at will by the colonizers (Gebara 2003). The global ecofeminist analysis and actions were a combination of those from the North and South, with scientific, social, political and religious vantage points.

Within the move towards a global ecofeminism, particular topics were examined from an ecofeminist viewpoint. Often it was the passionate concerns of individuals that brought particular issues or specific analyses to the ecofeminist intersection. Carol Adams was the primary leader in bringing animal rights into the ecofeminist arena. The issues of meat-eating, the international fur industry, experimentation on animals, and the sexualizing and feminizing of animals, discussed in her book *The Sexual Politics of Meat* (1994), made an impact within the ecological-feminist conversations. These kinds of associations were challenging, as not all ecofeminists or environmentalists are vegetarian, nor deeply concerned with animal troubles or suffering.

Local and global justice concerns such as land claims, nuclear power, militarism, education, abortion and cross-cultural issues were appearing on ecofeminist pathways. At times ecofeminism illuminated an issue and was transformative; at other times it seemed inadequate and politically ineffective in front of large global issues such as corporate globalization (Eaton 2000: 41–55).

In support of a growing global ecofeminist consciousness, national organizations emerged or reshaped themselves to be ecofeminist in orientation, such as Development Alternatives with Women for a New Era (DAWN) in Fiji, Women's Environment and Development Organization (WEDO) in New York, and Women, Environment, Education and Development (WEED) in Toronto. As a result of the United Nations Earth Summit in 1992, the theme of Women for a Healthy Planet and *Women's Action Agenda '21* were promoted internationally and became the impetus for countless local activist and education groups to appear around the world. The international web of relations and communications among ecofeminists is inestimable. Large institutions such as The United Nations Development Fund for Women, the World Bank, and the World Council of Churches also see the value, necessity and wisdom of ecofeminism. In addition there are innumerable local communities connecting women and ecological issues, as well as websites, newsletters, networks, and small organizations.

Summary
All of this activity is slowly moving the multitude of concerns of the ecofeminist agenda forward, and into cultural awareness and activities. This brief overview of the history and development of ecofeminism indicates that there are many paths into the women-nature, ecological feminist connection. Ecofeminism has quickly become a multidisciplinary and increasingly international insight. It is an intersection point, where those with deep concerns for the world can find comrades and allies, and indeed challenges. Its history and development is one way to appreciate the scope of this lively phenomenon called 'ecofeminism'.

Ecofeminism: Contributions and Congestion

Ecofeminism was exciting! Ecofeminism was an insight that proved to be useful, illuminating and instructive. Although it meant different things to different people, the ecological-feminist connection was valuable. It crystallized what people were doing and thinking, and propelled them to take seriously the cross-over between ecological and feminist issues. People came together from many directions, learning from each other and collaborating. For some, it was a new idea, a fresh insight, and a helpful tool. For others it confirmed their work in political, social and environmental movements. Ecofeminism became a way of seeing aspects of the world, of analysing certain problems, and of finding solutions. It also provided necessary resources from the past that helped the present and shaped the future. By 2000 ecofeminism was known in most Euro-western universities, and in many environmental and women's movements.

There is an ongoing evolution to ecofeminism, and a dynamic dialectic within its development. The activism has inspired the conceptual work, and the conceptual work has offered a solid base for the activism. From the 1970s to the present it has gathered form and energy, and moved continually into more disciplines, perspectives, and cultures. The history of ecofeminism is similar to people converging at a main crossroads. Ecofeminism is the totality of the various pathways to that point, the many conversations taking place on the way and the exchanges at the crossroads.

Ecofeminist Analyses: Empirical and Cultural-symbolic Approaches
As ecofeminism was developing, there became two particularly well-travelled directions from which to come. It is really two types of analyses that examine

differing aspects of the feminist-ecological intersection. One could be called
an empirical approach, and the other is a cultural-symbolic or conceptual
approach. While the division is artificial, it allows us to grasp a distinction that
has become important in ecofeminist conversations.

Empirical Approaches
The empirical approach is based on daily, material and lived experiences of
women. It addresses the fundamental realities of women and the earth systems
in which they live. As ecological crises worsen and multiply, daily living
becomes harder, especially for women. The availability of food, water, and a
decent agricultural base is diminishing, and it requires more time and effort to
meet the needs of a family. Women, often the custodians of the land, live this
increased harshness all the time. It also refers to the issues of women in
industrialized countries, where access to clean water is increasingly difficult,
where cancers, respiratory illnesses and a host of environmental sicknesses are
affecting a large proportion of people. Empirical data means that the source of
the analysis is as concrete as possible.

The empirical approach is also about examining the patterns causing these
conditions, such as deforestation, water contamination and corporate control
of common land. Connections are made between daily lived realities and the
larger forces causing increased stress and suffering. It is about connecting environmental illness to pesticides, and to government policies on or subsidizing of
pesticide use. The empirical ecofeminist work is that of an analysis of agency,
meaning data on the who, what, why, where and the how of the local and
global socio-ecological crises. The interlocking crises facing women and the
natural world are examined through issues of access to power and decision-
making.

Concerns about the international economic system, trade, militarism, development and consumerism, within contexts of growing social instability, ecological
ruin, environmental refugees, and the desperate life conditions of women, pre-
occupy this work. The empirical approach examines these socio-political and
economic structures, which restrict many women's lives to poverty, ecological
deprivation and economic powerlessness. In addition to research and analysis
that brings these issues forward, this work is about transforming these realities.

Cultural-Symbolic Approaches
The cultural-symbolic or conceptual approaches have been referred to as ecofeminist theory. It asserts that women and nature have been associated historically and conceptually, and that these ideas are ingrained within Euro-western
worldviews. Seeking the roots of the ecological crisis and misogyny (the hatred

of women), and their entwined linkages are central to ecofeminist *theory*. The historical coupling of the 'feminizing' of nature and the 'naturalizing' of women has led to a mutually reinforcing domination of both. The result is that men are understood to have innate power over both women and nature, and therefore the dominations of women and nature are justified and appear as 'natural'.

At the conceptual level ecofeminism includes, to varying degrees, in-depth analyses of culture: the different physical, psychological, social, economic, scientific, and religious presuppositions of what is true, appropriate and moral. It includes examining the symbols underlying all relationships within human societies, and human-natural world relations. The discovery of ecofeminism is that domination, as a mode of relating, is pervasive in many cultures, and is represented in social patterns including those of family relations, sexuality, education, governance, economic control, and ecological customs. A gender-nature association is often present, although the patterns are distinct depending on the culture, context and time period. This work reveals the values and assumptions hidden within a cultural worldview. Ecofeminist theory also envisions alternative philosophical and social conceptual frameworks based on benign human and human–earth relations, rather than on mutually supporting systems of domination.

Combined Analyses

Ecofeminist efforts at both the cultural-symbolic and socio-economic levels were mutually challenging. Those working mostly at a theoretical level were critiqued for ignoring the severe realities of women in impoverished or disempowered circumstances. The material local and global issues were slow to become integral to ecofeminist concerns, but found their place within the flow of traffic. People began to work more closely together, and although there are still blind spots, they do mutually inform and empower each other. This was neither an easy nor a straightforward task.

These two pathways, empirical and cultural-symbolic, represent confluences of other pathways into the ecofeminist roundabout. For example, some come to ecofeminism through the roadways of religion, by the cultural symbolic concepts of women and nature, while others come via religious social movements and activism as a result of specific issues. Scientists may come to the ecofeminist intersection through biotechnology, or through a feminist philosophy of science. Academics of all kinds may come through studies of global feminism, or cultural-symbolic ecofeminist theories. Activists often come through specific issues. Distinct cultures, different issues, separate analytic tools, and the uniqueness of each context means that ecofeminism in one place is not the same as in another. In addition, women experience domination differently, and from this difference emerges particular perspectives on the degradation of nature. Someone from Canada may come to ecofeminism through spirituality while another through the loss of a family farm to agribusiness. A woman living in Germany may respond with economic or scientific arguments and statistical evidence to the perceived environmental threat of nuclear weapons, while one living in the Narmada Valley in India may be prepared to sacrifice her life to stop a projected dam flooding her home and forcing her family to leave their native surroundings.

Given this diversity of content and context, ecofeminist positions resist any one or universalizing approach to human and/or ecological problems. What makes ecofeminism *feminist* is the commitment to the recognition and elimination of male-gender bias and the development of practices, policies and theories that do not reflect this bias. What makes ecofeminism *ecological* is an understanding of and commitment to the valuing and preserving of ecosystems, broadly understood. Karen Warren summarizes: 'any feminism which is not informed by ecological insights, especially women-nature insights, and any environmental philosophy which is not informed by ecofeminist insights is simply inadequate' (Warren 1994: 2). Far from being reductionist or simplistic, ecofeminism is a textured field of theoretical and experiential insights, encompassing different forms of knowledge, and embodied in the particular.

Feminism is a lens through which virtually all human activities can be examined. Ecofeminism is the convergence of feminist and ecological movements, and a logical extension of each. As each develops, new insights and knowledge are brought into the ecofeminist intersection. Yet neither the feminist nor ecological movements are uniform. Ecofeminism represents many kinds of feminist and ecological viewpoints.

Feminism(s) in Ecofeminism
Feminism is a challenge to patriarchy (rule of the father) and androcentrism, (male-centred values, beliefs and practices). Both are embedded in Euro-western worldviews and cultural practices, and prior to feminism they were accepted as normal, natural and even God-given. Feminism confronts patriarchy and androcentrism, revealing the bias against women. It brings forth values and structures that support women's equality and autonomy. Feminists, however, while wanting a better life for women, do not agree on the same analysis or vision of the future.

Feminists vary on what kind of world is desirable, and, how much and what kind of freedom is needed for women. They disagree on political strategies. Liberal feminists are often content with women's equal access to the current cultural and economic system. Socialist feminists want more substantial changes to the economic system to eliminate discrimination based on class and ethnicity. Radical feminists connect gender domination with all other forms of domination, and want changes at the cultural-symbolic and the empirical levels. Radical means to the root. Postmodern feminists can tolerate great divergences among feminists, provided each group can self-define with full autonomy. Some feminists are essentialist, meaning they believe that women possess inherent traits such as caring or co-operative skills, and others oppose shared characteristics for all women. Some include, or make pivotal, concerns for specific cultural groups, such as ethnicity. Some feminists see freedom predominantly in lesbian relations or women-oriented cultures. Still others are aware of the process of cultural and economic colonization, and stand for a postcolonial world and radical cultural freedom. Within this spectrum, spirituality is at times central, peripheral or irrelevant for individuals or groups. To further complicate this, many feminists have a combination of these tendencies, positions and commitments. Feminists who embrace ecological issues bring all these variations with them!

Ecology in Ecofeminism

Ecological issues are also understood from many vantage points and with a range of ecological paradigms that are fondly called from 'light' to 'dark' green. Light green means an anthropocentric paradigm, wherein humans are the most important species and other life forms and earth's matter can be used as resources for human well-being. Ecological problems are redressed by good stewardship and better management of the earth's resources. Dark green paradigms consider the whole earth to be important. All life forms need to flourish within the sophisticated and complex interconnected ecosystems. These non-anthropocentric paradigms are called biocentric, bioregional, ecocentric, whole earth systems, Gaia, deep ecology or cosmology. In between light and dark green are viewpoints that connect ecological ruin to social tension and injustice, such as social ecology, ecojustice, or green socialism. Each viewpoint emphasizes or values particular aspects, and some are mixtures. In addition, all of these distinctions refer to differing political strategies for environmental changes.

Which Ecofeminism and Going in What Direction?

Ecofeminism represents countless combinations of the distinct strands of feminism and different ecological viewpoints. From the beginning, those who accepted that feminist theory and practice must include an ecological perspective

and that solutions to ecological problems must include feminist analyses, dis-
agreed as to the nature of these connections. As ecofeminist philosopher Karen
Warren writes:

> ...the varieties of ecofeminism reflect not only the differences in the analysis of
> the woman/nature connection, but also differences on such fundamental matters
> as the nature of and the solutions to women's oppression, the theory of human
> nature, and the conceptions of freedom, equality, epistemology on which various
> feminist theories depend. (Warren 1987: 4)

Those who committed themselves to ecofeminism wrestled with the range of
issues and concepts that had gathered at the ecofeminist intersection. Although
both a historical and cross-cultural connection, some claim this women-
nature link should be deconstructed and contested. It has not served either
women or the earth. Others say it should be reclaimed, reworked, celebrated
and honoured. Still others consider it to be part of past histories rather than of
present relevance.

By the 1990s several specific tensions had emerged. It was not clear that
everyone was going in the same direction on the ecofeminist roundabout. In
depth ecofeminist research revealed the extent to which Euro-western cultures
were rooted in ideologies of domination, a central one being the interconnected domination of women and nature. While this work exposed the
ideological substructure of the problem, it was not straightforward to know
how to change it. A tension existed between those who developed ecofeminist
theories and those working for political change in social movements. Some
ecofeminists seemed to be more interested in the historical and symbolic
connections between women and nature, or sophisticated theories of how the
world should be, than the actual suffering of women and ecosystems. Others
perceived the greatest need to be in addressing economic and material realities,
and concrete issues of women's poverty and ecological stress. How was there
to be a relationship between those providing historical and theoretical analysis,
and those resisting pollution, loss of agricultural land or biodiversity decreases?
As Rosemary Radford Ruether stated, activists and academics need to work
together. She points out that the cultural-symbolic level of the relationship
between sexism and ecological exploitation is the ideological superstructure
that reflects and sanctions the social, economic, political and religious order
(Ruether 1996: 5). At times correctives are needed for the myopias which
plague ecofeminisms that emerge from white affluent or academic contexts.
Ecofeminists who draw primarily from those whose frameworks do not
recognize those at the bottom of the socio-economic system; they perpetuate

these myopias and contribute to an ecofeminism that is primarily cultural escapism rather than liberatory.

It became evident that ecofeminism as a whole was inconsistent. For some, ecofeminism was so broad and carried so many issues that it became haphazard. Others were frustrated with the inner contradictions. The discomfort with ecofeminism became an explicit focus of conversation. Academics examined ecofeminist theories, assumptions and particular interests. Although the original insights of the connections between the domination and exploitation of women and the earth was the basis of all ecofeminist research and practice, distinctions, disagreement and contradictions were evident. Feminists and ecofeminists reflected differently on the relationships between women and the natural world, and misogyny and the ecological crisis. Some ecofeminists concentrated more on women's issues than environmental problems, and others the reverse. Spirituality was central to some ecofeminists, for others it was irrelevant or aroused suspicion. Some found the diversity unmanageable, and wanted ecofeminism to contain specific ideas and orientations. Some fear that ecofeminism might be ineffective because of these variations and inconsistencies. Others rejoiced in the multitude of voices, celebrating the differences and disagreements. They encouraged such heterogeneity, including the contradictions, because diversity most reflects basic truths about the earth community. Some kept the ecology-feminist connection but changed the words, using phrases such as feminist ecology, feminist social ecology, feminist green socialism, feminist environmentalism, and feminist analyses of the environmental crisis.

Was ecofeminism as global as it seemed, or was it a North American/ Atlantic discussion that did not consider the women-nature reality in other parts of the world? North Americans often seem oblivious to many other different cultures and viewpoints. The women-nature connection and the ecological and feminist movements are not the same everywhere, and ecofeminism will be unique, or perhaps irrelevant, in other places. Lois Ann Lorentzen and myself discovered that ecofeminism operates differently in Christianity than in Buddhism, and in Kenya than in Chiapas, and in some places does not work at all (Eaton and Lorentzen 2003).

Discussions emerged around some early ecofeminist claims that there is a natural or essential affiliation between women and the earth. Some felt that women are closer to nature than men due to menstruation and childbirthing. Others thought that it was 'natural' for women to be caring, kind, communal and relational, and thus their concern for the earth was a logical extension of a caring nature. These ecofeminists celebrated the connection between women and nature, and while opposing their mutual domination, kept the belief that women are more linked to nature than men. This essentialism was adamantly refuted by other ecofeminists. They wanted to dismantle the connection saying there is no special women-nature link, and argued that to maintain the link is to maintain the mutual domination. The combination of ecofeminism, essentialism and religion or spirituality was particularly troublesome. For those who reject essentialism, this combination caused an uncritical rejection of religion or spirituality as well. This limited the availability of space for religious voices within some ecofeminist conversations, and at times discredited ecofeminism. By the mid 1990s essentialism had faded from most ecofeminist discussions.

Some ecofeminist spiritualities were criticized for ignoring social, cultural and historical contexts. They were challenged to move beyond beautiful ideas of how the world could be to examine the social structures of domination such as industrialism, militarism and male consciousness. Ecofeminist spiritualities were feared to be ineffective if political transformation was not central, or seen as primarily an internal and individual change of consciousness, rather than collective action in social and political processes.

Ecofeminism was thought by some to be hopelessly idealistic by celebrating the beauty and dignity of women and the earth while seemingly ignorant of the social, political and economic systems that perpetuated women's poverty and ecological ruin. It was seen as too spiritual, too theoretical or too apolitical to be effective. There were some scathing critiques, such as that of social ecologist Janet Biehl in *Finding Our Way: Rethinking Ecofeminist Politics* (1991).

Conclusion: A Way Out

Evaluation of the breadth of ecofeminism reveals many voices, theoretical positions, practices and political leanings. Foundational assumptions differ, as do determining the pivotal issues. The goals and means to achieve them are divergent. People come to ecofeminism from a variety of routes and take it in multiple directions. Many use the term, and from distinct vantage points. It is new and flexible, and no one controls the definitions. Carolyn Merchant suggests there are no less than five categories of ecofeminism: liberal, cultural, social, socialist, and women in the Third World (1992). There are undoubtedly more.

Objections to elements within ecofeminism have furthered discussions, encouraged a broadening of concerns and promoted a healthy and lively dialogue. During a phase of ecofeminism's history, this yielded to a trend where vast amounts of energy were consumed in conceptual debates while crucial problems worsened. In the words of Marti Kheel, an early patron of ecofeminism: 'It is a sad irony that the destruction of the natural world appears to be proceeding in direct ratio to the construction of moral theories for how we should behave in light of this plight' (Kheel 1991: 62). Nonetheless the continuing conversation surrounding ecofeminism is beneficial for theoretical lucidity and to persist in connecting of social, political and ecological issues and praxis.

As each pathway enters the ecofeminist intersection, it develops a definition. There are a lot from which to choose! Ruether describes ecofeminism as the 'symbolic and social connections between the oppression of women and the domination of nature', grounded in a union between the radical ecology movement and feminism (Ruether 1991: 1). Anne Primavesi characterizes ecofeminism as the bringing of an ecological paradigm into play from a feminist perspective, setting out to disclose the intrinsic link in male-dominated cultures between how one speaks about women and nature, and how one behaves towards them (Primavesi 1991: 36). From ecofeminist philosophy comes an understanding that it is a convergence of ecology and feminism into 'a new social theory and political movement [which] challenges gender relations, social institutions, economic systems, sciences, and views of our place in the biosphere' (Lahar 1991: 28). I refer to ecofeminism as a lens through which all disciplines are examined and refocused (Eaton 1998: 57–82). Charlene Spretnak claims that 'ecofeminists address the crucial issues of our time, from reproductive technology to Third World development, from toxic poisoning to the vision of a new politics and economics – and much more' (Spretnak 1990: 8–9).

To fully explore ecofeminism, several disciplines are needed, such as a team of the following:

> ...historians of culture, natural scientists and social economists who all share a concern for the interconnection between the domination of women and exploitation of nature. It needs visionaries to image how to construct a new socio-economic system and a new cultural consciousness that would support relations of mutuality rather than competitive power. For this one needs poets, artists and liturgists, as well as revolutionary organizers, to incarnate more life-giving relationships in our cultural consciousness and social system. (Ruether 1991: 2)

In the light of this diversity, and of the fact that today some ecofeminist groups can communicate instantly with others through Internet links, any categorization has to be provisional.

Ecofeminism is interdisciplinary, international and politically active. It connects women from around the world. Although ecofeminism is not a mass movement, it is becoming a third wave of feminism and represents a new social theory and political movement. Ecofeminism is about social, political, spiritual, economic and ecological transformation. It is analysis, critique, vision, and action, transforming the forms and patterns of relationships between women and men, between diverse cultures, between people and animals, and between humans and the larger earth community. Lively debates continue around ecofeminism as trans-cultural or context specific, between theory and social transformation, and in international conversations about democracy, globalization, dreams of a harmonious past or future, spiritualities, and essentialism. Many women and men, inspired by ecofeminism, are involved in projects to improve their part of the world. In general, ecofeminism is about a desire to heal the wounds caused by the splits between nature and culture, mind and body, women and men, reason and emotion, spirit and matter, theory and action, and ultimately between humans and the earth.

Chapter Two

The Quest for Origins: In the Beginning...

Ecofeminism claims that there is a historical and contemporary connection between women and the natural world, that is both empirical and cultural-symbolic. They also claim that this women-nature link is one of the causes of the pervasive domination of women and the destruction of the earth, and that their mutual oppressions are interlocked. This chapter looks at the cultural-symbolic claim. It begins with an overview of the historical and conceptual links between women and nature in Euro-western heritage.

Women and Nature: An Overview

An age-old association between women and nature, or women and the earth, has existed in many cultures, and continues to do so. There is evidence that for millennia women and the earth were seen as those who generated life. Women mysteriously birthed children. The earth provided the possibilities of food, shelter, pleasure, and adventure as well as ultimately overtaking human life with death. At times the women-nature link appears as a favourable and advantageous affiliation while at other times adverse and injurious. Women have been perceived of as nurturing, selfless, strong, selfish, feeble, sexual or asexual. Nature, meaning all that is not human, has undergone similar shifts in perception, accepted at times as providing, nourishing, and bountiful or as chaotic, dangerous and sparse. This usually depends on which culture, during which epoch and using which historical sources. It is impossible to track all of these historical shifts, or even to know how historical records were lived out concretely.

In-depth multicultural research and case studies of the history of the connection between women and nature are only beginning. It seems that in most parts of the world, historically and in many places today, there is some form of a women/nature nexus that deeply influences beliefs, attitudes and actions. It is not known for certain if, how, when and where this nexus emerged in each context. Were these the ideas of the elite men about how they wanted to order the world, or was this the operative worldview of most of the people in all regions? It is difficult to know much with any accuracy. It is also uncertain if, how and where it is related to current practices and problems surrounding women and the natural world. Ecofeminist research has shown that, when present, the women/nature nexus is varied and functions distinctly in different cultures and contexts (Eaton and Lorentzen 2003).

Nonetheless, it is central to understand that for Euro-western societies there was a decided shift in the way that women and nature were associated together. The ecofeminist claim is that this connection is central to women's oppression and ecological ruin. This negative women-nature correlation became established within Euro-western worldviews and has specific roots in the philosophical, religious and scientific developments. Ecofeminists claim that the past history of the nexus sheds light on the present-day relationship between the oppression of women and ecological devastation. The following discussion is related only to these developments in Euro-western societies and those influenced by them through colonization and globalization.

The Domination of Women

Beliefs about the World: Hierarchical Dualisms
According to ecofeminists, Euro-western cultures developed beliefs that the world was divided dualistically and hierarchically. This is a worldview, and one that masquerades as truth. Dualistic conceptual structures or bipolar frameworks are a manner of thinking in pairs or opposites, with one side having a priority over the other. To perceive differences in pairs, such as day/night, left/-right or up/down, is not necessarily a problem. It is when pairs are considered as opposites or polarities, and not just as different, that causes the trouble. For example, the following pairs are also considered to be opposites:

woman	man
feminine	masculine
the body	the mind
emotion	reason
sexuality	chastity
earth	heaven
nature	culture
matter	spirit
demonic	divine
inferior	superior

In dualisms such as these the second or 'superior' column is given priority over the first, thus they are hierarchical dualisms. Not only are the second pairs preferable, they are considered to be the norm; that which most represents an unblemished world and a perfect human. Everything is measured against the characteristics and values of the superior column, such that it dominates over the inferior one. In addition, each column is internally connected, meaning that women are considered to be inherently correlated to 'the feminine'; their bodies, emotions, sexuality, earth, nature and matter, and together these are inferior to the superior column. Life is ordered according to these views. They combine into a conceptual framework, ideology or worldview that is reflected in social practices. It is important to understand that these are beliefs, not truths. For example, what constitutes a 'woman' in these beliefs is an abstraction or hypothetical ideal, and does not represent the medley of actual women. The same is true for what is a 'man' and the internal associations of the superior column apply to men. Both are then imposed on real women and men, who are influenced to act accordingly. Both women and men are limited by these dualisms. One crucial difference is that it is men – not all of course – who have determined these ideals, and in general it works in their favour. This worldview makes male power over both women and nature appear to be righteous, even required, and thus justified.

Ecofeminists refer to these pairings as hierarchical dualisms. They claim this manner of thinking points to a logic of domination entrenched in Euro-western history and worldview (Warren 1990: 133). It is an implicit belief system, meaning it is so pervasive that it is taken for granted and unquestioned. Religion, philosophy, science and cultural symbols share these beliefs and reinforce this worldview. Social patterns including education, governance, economic control and socio-sexual norms reflect this logic of domination.

Some examples may help illustrate how these dualisms still function today. Until recently in most countries it has been acceptable, even desirable, that women receive less education than men, talk less in public, own less or no property, are given to their husbands or take their husbands' name in marriage, receive lesser salaries for equivalent work, choose predominantly caring professions rather than political careers, etc. Women are considered to be mothers by nature, and thus their place is first and foremost in the home. Women work in the sphere of nature – the home – where their caring, emotions and body (pregnancy, breastfeeding and child-rearing) are central. Women are rarely socialized to feel that all options are open to them, even if legally there are many possibilities. In most societies still today, there are varieties of controls around sexuality and intimate relationships for women, in both subtle and blatant forms. For example, although romanticized often in films and media, the idealized love relationship, chiefly women with men, usually requires a loss of independence for the woman and where her life-reference is 'her man'. In some places the 'ideal' woman is sexually savvy, professionally capable, and yet knows her place in the relationship. In other places, the 'ideal' woman is sexually pure, perhaps covered to various degrees, likely subservient to men, and also 'knows her place' in relationships. In Northern countries and major urban centres there is a huge and insidious fashion industry that shapes girls' self esteem to be dependent on male approval. It has meant that females are often subtly affirmed as sexual objects for men, in dress and demeanor. Blatantly, the pornography business, the international trafficking in women and girls, prostitution and sexual slavery are quite prevalent, and more so than many want to know about. Feminists and ecofeminists make it their business to bring these realities to consciousness. Although much has been gained for women in many parts of the world, with colossal efforts for several centuries in a painful dance of progress and regress, much more needs to happen. These facts, and the endless list of fights for women's rights, begs the question of the origins and historical roots of domination of women, and a quest for the origins of patriarchy.

The Quest for Origins
The search for the origins of these problems is imperative for ecofeminists attempting to understand the foundations that generated such an extensive and historical asymmetry between women and men. It is also relevant because the associations between women and nature, and men and culture are very hard to change and often seem intransigent. The research on origins is important for at least five reasons. One is to refute any belief, biological reductionist, or essentialist argument that men are inherently superior to women. A second is that the historical roots of the mutual dominations of women and the natural world reveal foundational assumptions about both that need to be contested. A third is to bring to consciousness and moral awareness the atrocious history of women's oppression such that current practices can be more effectively prevented. A fourth is to uncover the causes of the excessive ecological destruction of some societies, and to attempt to reverse this trend. And fifth, this theoretical research exposes hidden tentacles of a worldview of domination that continues to be operative.

This task is not simple. Some of these origins go back many centuries beyond substantial records, and even into early human settlements. Given the urgency of the contemporary crises, such work may seem abstract and secondary. The aim, however, is not to produce disengaged research but an attempt to use the past to transform the present. It is part of a political strategy for emancipation. Some even claim that it is not possible to overcome the current situation without understanding the foundation and the functioning of the past legacy (Mies 1988: 67).

There are two aspects to this quest for origins. One is to understand the affiliations between women and nature, or women and the earth. The second is to grasp how this is linked to practices of domination, such that domination became a way of ordering the world. Together these two aspects, discussed in turn, are part of the onset of women's subjugation and a predacious approach towards the earth. Ecofeminists claim that since both are endemic to patriarchy, a brief look at its origin will be useful.

The Emergence of Patriarchy
The origin of social domination is enigmatic. What is definite is that ideologies and social constructions of domination are core to civilizations that are patriarchal, that is where the father rules. With the exception of a few insular communities, patriarchy is the social structure everywhere in the world. Yet little is known for certain about the inception of patriarchy. It is a form of social arrangement that emerged between five and ten thousand years ago and in different parts of the world. Patriarchy assumes male supremacy (androcentrism), but the specific form of androcentrism and ensuing female subservience has never been identical in every region, kinship, ecological setting, ethnographic grouping, or class structure. Usually patriarchy is kept intact through elite males, while many groups of men are considered inferior – not to women – but to the ruling men. Nevertheless an asymmetry between men and women that is symbolically, socially, sexually and materially codified with male dominance is the recurrent pattern of development. Patriarchy/androcentrism is an omni-cultural phenomenon, from the earliest forms of human social arrangements to the present. Androcentrism, according to Vandana Shiva is 'the oldest of oppressions' (Shiva 1988: 3) and thought by some to be the root cause of all dominations (Doubiago 1990: 43; King 1990: 106–107).

Patriarchy often provides socio-biological or biological arguments for the oppression of women and an explanation for gender inequalities. For example, women are designed for child-rearing not politics. Women are the weaker sex. They are vulnerable and need protecting. Women are smaller, shorter, have less upper body strength and are more emotional than men, thus are inferior to men. Yet in reality women have greater overall endurance and stamina than most men. While the ideology of men is such that women need protecting, it is men who attack women. Feminists reject any worldview, belief or assumption that considers women to be innately inferior to men. Instead they turn to varieties of social theories to explain the presence of patriarchy and gender inequality.

Many have explored how and why patriarchy and male supremacy became such a global social and symbolic structure, and multiple theories are offered. Gerda Lerner suggests that patriarchy emerged due to a complex combination of the following: learning and organizing agricultural techniques, invasions, the stealing of wealth and war spoils (which were women, slaves and items), the solidifying of class power and political elites, and the realization that strength and domination are effective tools and weapons (Lerner 1986). Others consider that population pressures, ecological scarcity, patrilinear inheritance, property rights, economic want or abundance, reproduction and child-rearing practices, bio-psychological influences, colonization, and inter-social exchanges are all implicated in the emergence of the patriarchal social configuration. Some evidence indicates that the earliest forms of human slavery were of women. This later congealed into generic master-slave structures between men and women, ethnic superiority and human–earth relations. However, none of these theories fully explain the supremacy of male valour, ultimacy of male qualities and activities, the need for male offspring, the emergence of male societies, and the virtually exclusive male political and economic control. The male supremacy complex interacts with every thread in the fabric of social life, and cannot be explained with any one theory (Coontz and Henderson 1986: 32).

Matriarchy and the Goddess

A few feminists and ecofeminists maintain that prior to the full institutionalization of patriarchy some women held positions of authority, exercised great personal and social power and enjoyed greater freedom than most women experience under patriarchy (Stone 1978; Eisler 1987; Gimbutas 1991). There is evidence to suggest that Goddess cultures predated patriarchy and the worship of male divine images. It is plausible that these were mutually reinforcing circumstances; meaning a connection between the worship of Goddesses and the heightened status of women. This interpretation is based on three key facts: (1) Evidence of matrilineal descent, which is assumed to point to an ancient matriarchy or at least an equality with men; (2) A plethora of ancient goddesses, women-centred myths, female religious artifacts, and priestess-led temples, which are assumed to reveal societies where women held central leadership positions or had great freedom; (3) Elaborate women's burial sites, that may indicate equal status with leading men. These facts and artifacts exist, in some areas in abundance. The question is: What do they mean? Facts rarely give away the interpretations laden upon them. For many the meaning of this evidence is uncertain at best. For example, matrilineage continues to exist in patriarchal societies, such as Spain, parts of the Middle East, and Quebec. Hindu Goddesses thrive in patriarchal India. Gender segregation does not necessarily imply oppression, and finally ruling women do not reveal an absence of patriarchy.

The debate continues as to how to interpret these indicators (Eller 2000). There is evidence to suggest that patriarchy caused a loss of privilege, power and prestige for some women in some places, and may even have overturned a few egalitarian societies. For now I accept the arguments that this is not sufficient to claim a matriarchal or matrifocal stage of human history, or that in most places patriarchy supplanted societies where gender equity and Goddesses had flourished. The predecessors of patriarchy are simply not known.

What can be known about early human communities is that the gender relations were complex and differentiated. With the rise of patriarchy comes the solidification of elite male rule, which results in a definition, and then negation, of what is labeled as feminine, hence female. However, the precise origins of male dominance, sanctified by patriarchal ideologies and myths, and the ensuing systemic oppression of women, are shrouded in an inaccessible past.

The Origins of Domination
A question of interest to ecofeminists is: Of what does domination consist? Domination is a pervasive ideology and practice, certainly in gender relations, but also related to ethnicity, class, culture, and the natural world. The practice of domination and oppression has identifiable roots in hierarchy, misogyny, androcentrism, anthropocentrism, and in the origins of organized agriculture (Lerner 1986: 48–53). Some ecofeminists consider hierarchy to be the prototype/archetype of oppression. Ecofeminist theologian Anne Primavesi observes that hierarchy is embedded deeply in cultural consciousness and is an integral component of the development of extended modes of domination. (Primavesi 1992: 195–221). Elizabeth Dodson Gray also makes a case for the intimate familiarity with hierarchical processes from the personal to the political levels. The manner in which we conceptualize and actualize cultural practices is permeated with hierarchical beliefs and structures (Gray 1979).

Other ecofeminists see misogyny (the hatred of women) in addition to androcentrism, to be the foundational form of domination and the origin of the cultural distortions. Androcentrism needs to be differentiated from misogyny, although the two are connected. Androcentrism constitutes the ideologies and social patterns that require a sexual division of labour, economic privilege for men, and where women may have some, but not full, social access. Androcentrism is often found under the guise of 'women and men are equal but different.' This familiar concept usually translates into men deciding what this difference is and how it will be lived, which inevitably is oppressive to women as their lives and freedom are limited. Misogyny is an ideology that leads to the overt domination of women, often in forms of preventing food or education, in sexual slavery or as property, treating women with contempt, and denigrating women's lives, contributions and potential. Androcentrism and misogyny can be difficult to disentangle, and perhaps they are the same poison in different toxic dosages.

Certainly misogyny is not the only form of domination, but it is extensive and has penetrated to all levels of social formation. To determine whether misogyny or hierarchy is the ultimate paradigm of domination would be difficult to substantiate. The complex systems of domination in existence, including heterosexism, ethnocentrism, cultural imperialism, global capitalism, and political and religious structures lend themselves to the treatment of lives as commodities. They have intensely hierarchical and symbolic systems of legitimation. All have both misogynist and hierarchical aspects. It is more useful to consider a dialectic existing between misogyny and hierarchy.

An affiliated question about domination as a mode of relating surrounds the relationship between androcentrism and anthropocentrism or human-centredness. A conceptual link between the two has been the basis of many ecofeminist arguments. Warren has argued that patriarchy is both andro- and anthropocentric. It contains a conceptual framework that subordinates both women and nature by naturalizing women, feminizing nature and assuming that both are inferior (Warren 1988). A question to be pondered is whether nature is devalued by virtue of a perceived association with women, or the reverse. While the ecological movement has made the notion of anthropocentrism its flagship, ecofeminism pushes for an androcentric critique to be taken seriously. These discrepancies can be dividing points among ecological schools of thought.[1]

Again the quest for specific origins is thwarted by the past and the complexity of the question. From the present moment we can trace back these

---

1.   A major distinction among ecological schools is the centrality and understanding of the critique of anthropocentrism, which is related to the status given to the natural world concerning instrumental or intrinsic value. Yet neither social nor deep ecology, although basing their critiques on distinct analyses, has taken seriously the androcentrism of their positions.

concepts (misogyny, hierarchy, anthropocentrism) but the relationship between concepts and historical practices is ambiguous. Maria Mies, combining sociology and ecofeminism, traces the origins of the appropriation of nature and the hierarchical sexual division of labour to the earliest development of human communities. She suggests that in the study of the ongoing evolution of human nature, the development of gender differences, including the physiological dimensions, must be linked to the social dimension. She writes, 'men's/ women's human nature does not evolve out of biology in a linear, monocausal process, but is the result of the history of women's/men's interaction with nature and with each other' (Mies 1986: 49). Human history is social history, and humans produce their lives, and their ideas about life, in an historical process.

Most ecofeminists connect all these together within a logic of domination or a master-slave polemic that permeates much of Euro-western societies and elsewhere. These are systemic oppressions. Ecofeminists expose the attitudes and ideologies of master-slave dialectics that are lived out in myriad and seemingly endless variations. Since ecofeminism is dedicated to ferreting out the systemic logic of domination, these analyses of the origin of domination provide tools for recognizing and dismantling oppressive systems – theoretically at least.

To come at the women/nature nexus from the domination of women reveals many aspects as described above. Other dimensions are revealed when the starting point is the domination of nature.

The Domination of Nature

If we consider that the current ecological crises can be summarized as, at least in part, a problem of human domination of the natural world, then it is important to understand how this particular domination came to be. To begin we might ask: What is nature?

What is Nature?

Human perceptions of 'nature' are extremely varied, as are the variations within the natural world. The range of interpretations is very large, in keeping with an immense diversity of cultural contexts and bioregions of the earth. Season, climate, altitude, food availability, presence or absence of water, mammals, reptiles or insects that can or cannot co-exist with humans, and beauty, all influence the way human communities perceive of, evaluate and live within the rhythms, provisions and restraints of 'nature'. The Inuit have dozens of words for snow, but few for gradations of heat. Those who live in deserts, lush climates, or in turbulent weather systems all develop a language of intimacy with 'nature'.

'Nature' has collected a variety of other meanings that are more related to social theories than anything within the biotic world. For example, these days to claim a person is 'natural' could mean that she/he demonstrates proper behaviour and is 'normal', or is comfortable to be with, spontaneous or easy going. To do something because it is 'natural' can mean how it is supposed to be, or that it is effortless. We often hear about 'natural' instincts. Some women are said to possess 'natural' beauty. 'Natural' childbirth means no medication and no caesarean, or birth with a midwife and at home.

An object that is 'natural' might be clean, healthy or good. 'Natural' food usually meaning organic, raw, not processed, or chemical-free. Something that is not 'natural' could be inappropriate, unhealthy, manufactured or offensive. Each one of these usages is packed with intentions, value systems and preferences. Both 'natural' and its opposite, 'unnatural' have layers of meanings and judgements.

'Nature' is also 'outside', or a place where humans go to get away from cities, buildings, or institutionalized thought patterns – to get a break from it all. In this meaning 'nature' includes everything except humans. But not any place is 'nature', as it must be beautiful, green, somewhat manicured, and relatively tranquil. It may be an image of an untouched, unspoiled wilderness. Dense bush with wild boars and venomous snakes do not fit the bill! We go 'into nature' to be refreshed. People who live simply or choose it voluntarily are said to have 'returned to nature' or live 'close to nature'. Nature is characterized as both tame, ordered, and friendly, but at other times wild, chaotic and dangerous. Frequently nature is referred to as 'her'.

There is an assortment of other meanings attached to this word. Nature has been associated with freedom, adventure, spirituality, and wealth. Only the affluent can afford to be surrounded by 'nature's abundance and beauty'. Most car commercials present an isolated vista of beauty, solitude and untouched natural world – computer generated of course! 'Nature' is not found in crowded urban sprawls or garbage dumps.

There have been centuries of debates about nature versus nurture. What comes with the human package 'naturally' and what can be learned is divided into nature or nurture. In an associated manner 'nature' has also been contrasted with technology, culture or artificial creations. To go against 'nature' is to resist the innate direction of things. At times we must let 'nature take her course', which often refers to allowing death its due. To 'rise above nature' is to go beyond the inherent limits. It may mean to discipline one's self beyond elemental or even sordid desires. It may also mean to diminish bodily, emotional or sexual desires. To conquer nature is to have control and be free from what are considered to be unacceptable constraints.

Religions constantly use 'natural' and 'nature' for an infinite variety of claims. 'Nature' is seen to be permeated with the divine: a source of wonder, inspiration and presence. In Christianity nature can be both inspirational and in opposition to the divine or what is supernatural. Nature may be a subservient to or an incomplete stepping-stone to supernatural, depending on the conceptual package of 'natural' and 'supernatural'. In religion 'nature' usually needs to be corrected in one way or another. The 'laws of nature' and 'natural law' are minefields of religious concepts, biases, and instruments of social organization or control.

In Christianity, 'nature' is also a state of being, in opposition to a state of grace. Grace is, of course, better. Nature is outside the realm of miracles, which are in the domain of the supernatural, grace and salvation. The end result is that nature is a lesser reality than the divine, and nature needs correcting, elevating or redeeming. What is and is not 'of nature', 'natural', part of 'human nature' and women and men's 'nature' have been debated throughout recorded history.

These interpretations become powerful worldviews and mechanisms of social order and control. For example, in some societies beliefs about what is 'natural' is used to prevent girls from receiving an education, or freedom to vote, or food, or being confined to lives of endless childbearing and rearing, sexual slavery and early death. Many cultures are organized so that it is accepted as 'natural' for men to make decisions for women, to decide how they can dress and walk, with whom they can communicate and how, how they are to be punished, or to have sexual access at will, or even to rape. In biotechnology the 'nature' argument goes both ways: that it is both natural to manipulate genetic material, and natural to leave it alone. Thus to use the word nature or natural is to use an ambiguous and highly political word. These words are charged with mixed meanings and often used to justify ideologies, social theories, gender discrimination or fixed human–earth relationships.

When I use the term 'nature', I am referring to two realities. One is to address the *ideas* about 'nature'; religious, philosophical and social. The second usage is about nature as being the natural world. The term the 'natural world' refers to the earth and its biotic communities of life. Natural world and earth community are synonymous. The natural world is an evolving and mutually enhancing life-system that is intricate, delicately balanced, interdependent and immeasurably complex. The earth community is at least four billion years of age, always unfolding and transforming with drama and gracefulness in an elegant profusion of life.[2] The earth has brought forth a stunning array of life forms, including the dazzling and formidable dinosaurs. The evolutionary process is staggering. It suggests, for example, that whales are one of the oldest and most stable mammals alive today. Their history moves from sea to land, and then over millennia transforming from something like contemporary wolves back to the sea again. Humanity emerged from this earth community over a long genetic and ecological development from amoebas to apes, and in a process that was non-linear or by design. From my study of evolutionary history it is impossible to claim that the human is the only goal of this immense life-process.

I am using the term 'natural world' to refer to the earth's life systems and communities of beings and non-beings in an evolving and self-organizing whole.[3] Yet the natural world is not monolithic and contains innumerable varieties of ecosystems and life-forms. I am referring specifically to the multiple physical manifestations of life, their interactions, and systemic functioning. There is no 'environment' outside of the natural world, no nature other than the mix of life on earth.

Humans are fully a part of nature and earth's ecosystems, and are differentiated as a species but not as ontologically other than natural. Humans emerged from and are embedded in the natural world. Humanity, in my view, has no additional, other or superior 'nature', regardless of human pretense to the contrary. I, along with most ecofeminists, do not accept that nature and culture are intrinsically separate, in spite of the difficulties of separating the natural biotic world and the social constructions of it. What differentiates the human species from all other animals is a developed capacity for language, self-reflective consciousness, cultural and technological sophistication, and the only species to have spread into virtually every ecosystem. Humans are also

---

2.   In spite of its increasing popularity, I do not accept the creationist arguments that the earth is three or ten thousand years old, or that humanity did not evolve from within the complex life-thrust of the earth, or from primates. I consider the anti-evolution/creationism arguments to be intellectually and scientifically vacuous and based on a form of Christian fundamentalism and literalism, and other irrational foundations, even though it makes sense to adherents. For a representation of this discussion see Brian Alters and Sandra Alters, *Defending Evolution in the Classroom: A Guide to the Creation/Evolution Controversy* (2001); John Haught, *God After Darwin: A Theology of Evolution* (1999).

3.   For arguments in favour of understanding the earth as a whole system see James Lovelock, *The Ages of Gaia: A Biography of Our Living Planet* (1988); Elisabeth Sahtouris, *Earth Dance: Living Systems In Evolution* (2000), and *Gaia: The Human Journey from Chaos to Cosmos* (1989); and Anne Primavesi, *Sacred Gaia: Theology as Earth Science* (2000).

the only species that seems capable of endangering the very basis upon which it depends for survival; not a laudable trait for species endurance!

The Domestication of the Natural World

The quest for origins of the ecological crisis is challenging. All proponents within the radical ecological movements claim that the human community is excessively dominating the natural world. A viable human future is in jeopardy, and a viable and diverse earth community is deteriorating rapidly. There are two dimensions, at least, of the human–earth dialectic that are important. The first is the physical relationship between human survival and the natural world. The second is the history of how human cultures have interpreted the natural world. The ideas about the natural world legitimize the treatment of it and provide an explanation of the human role within the vastness of the natural world. The physical relationship and the ideas about the earth are intimately connected.

The Emergence of the Human

It is important not to be naive or romantic about a past where human–earth relations were in a state of perfect harmony. There was never an idyllic era where humans lived without an ecological impact or footprint. Humans have always survived by being a predator, vegetarian or otherwise, and have always taken what was needed from their ecosystems. This is true for all life-forms, and throughout the earth life exists in an infinite array of complex interactions; predatory-prey, mutually enhancing or symbiotic relations, and metabolic, molecular, and climactic exchanges. The difference between the past and the present is that humans have never had such capacity for a deleterious impact, and on such a scale. Many take far more than what is needed. A further problem is that the disregard for the destruction of the earth's life support systems and vast spectacle of life is both pragmatically absurd in the interests of survival, and pathologically indifferent to the diversity, beauty and wonder of the earth. Ecofeminists search for some understanding that will reveal how the present destructive human–earth relationships came into being.

Humans learned to survive on the fruits of the earth, with a gradual domestication of animals and plants, and with increasing capacity to collaborate with the earth's sophisticated life-systems. Apart from the very few hunter-gatherer communities still in existence, all human communities depend on organized agriculture to survive. This long history of mastery and manipulation of the earth has accelerated into the current critical juncture, where global agrobusiness, bio and genetic technologies, and an inability to live within the restraints and rhythms are deteriorating the very life-support systems of the planet. A brief glimpse at parts of the human domestication of nature helps us grasp the challenge humanity is facing.

During most of human existence, approximately two million years, survival depended upon gathering, herding and hunting. Although there is evidence of deliberate forest clearing by felling and fire as early as 30,000 years ago in New Guinea, it is only in the last few thousand years that several great ecological transitions have occurred. One of the most significant ecological transitions is the Neolithic Revolution; a combination of the domestication of agriculture, the growth of human settlements, and the beginning of religious and political elites. This revolution began as early as 10,000 BCE and was the norm by 5000 BCE. Feminists refer to this era as the rise of patriarchy.

Although the ecological history is sketchy, the shift from nomadic hunting and gathering to herding animals to organizing agriculture in settlements took place over several thousand years, unevenly but inevitably. The developments that occurred in significant and unrelated regions of the world, Southwest Asia and Mesopotamia, China and Mesoamerica, are fascinating. As early as 7500 BCE a village of twenty-five houses in Jarmo, Iran (now in Khuzistan), depended on an intensive system of mixed farming, domesticated barley, emmer and peas, herding sheep and goats, and rarely hunting (Ponting 1991: 45). Evidence of winter-grown wheat and barley was found in Ali Kosh, Iran in the period between 6000–5500 BCE. In China, the domestication of millet was established by 6000 and rice by 5000 BCE. In Mesoamerica the growing of peppers, squash, tomatoes, gourds and maize was organized by 5000 BCE (Ponting 1991: 53). This ability to domesticate and cultivate crops led to greater populations, settled societies, specializations, social stratifications, and religious and political elites. The administration and distribution of food came to be under the control of elites, and later of those most powerful to seize it.

From these origins came a history of increasingly sophisticated control over the natural world, mainly for food production and trade. During this time societies flourished and grew in population according to food production, and also declined, at times dramatically, with food shortages. Societies deteriorated and even disappeared due to deforestation, soil depletion or salination, and environmental decline since at least 1000 BCE. Over these centuries animals became extinct, such as elephants and giraffes from the Nile valley and the lion and leopard in Greece as early as 2350 BCE. By the year 1000 CE many if not most of the large animals everywhere had been severely depleted or were extinct, predominantly through human settlement. In spite of the ecological ebb and flow within the development of agriculture, and at times incredibly intricate agrarian systems such as in China, this ecological era was marked mainly with the need to survive and the establishment of human settlements. Then there was a distinct shift in human–earth relations from domestication to domination, from survival to savagery in Euro-western cultures.

Aggressive Plundering: Domination
The second dimension in the quest for the origins of the domination of nature is what human communities have *thought* about the natural world. From the earliest times to the present, humans have related to the natural world through ideas about it. Different regions and religions have radically different interpretations about the world. As mentioned, 'nature' has been conceived of as benevolent or threatening, nurturing or withholding, life-giving or life-taking, kind or harsh, spirit-filled or barren, divine or demonic. Humans, as social-symbolic creatures, relate to the earth through ideas or beliefs. Therefore the history of beliefs is significant as to how humans treat the earth.

Much of the thinking about the natural world is related to how humans understand themselves in relationship to the 'rest of nature'. In short, it is about humans. Are humans part of nature? Are we an integral part of the whole, partially of nature, or separate from it? How is this separation interpreted; superior, distinct, other, or inferior? How human societies have answered these questions is decisive to the legitimating of actions toward or manipulation of the earth. In Euro-western societies humans are usually understood to be not only distinct from the 'rest of nature', but also the supreme form of life.

Humans and other Animals
The gradual elimination of animals was extensive virtually everywhere there were human settlements, usually as a side effect of human development but increasingly due to hunting and commercial exploitation. The domestication and killing of animals for survival and land requisition was common in the Neolithic revolution. However a few records exist documenting the origins of the deliberate killing of animals for sport or just elimination.

The Roman Empire was addicted to the slaughter of animals for sport and ceremonies, such as the 9000 animals killed during the dedication ceremonies of the Coliseum in Rome (Ponting 1991: 158). The intentional massacre of animals became part of the ethos of European civilizations. The decimation of animals increased from 1300 to 1800 CE until most species were eliminated. The data around the warlike extermination of beavers, eagles, squirrels, migratory birds, herons, condors, fish, seals, otters, walruses, whales, and even sparrows, snails, wasps, ants and worms is shocking. Big game hunting in Africa and India devastated most mammal populations, and even more so in North America with the hunting of bison, horses, beavers, racoons and passenger pigeons. Markets were created for pelts of all kinds, and for feathers, horns, and hooves. Markets developed for many plants, such as orchids. The numbers of animals killed, not for survival but for a market economy or for sport, is in the billions. The ecological impact has been staggering. As early as 1200 CE there were relatively few large mammals or fur bearing animals left in Russia or Western Europe. The aggression was frenzied. For example, on Macquarie Island, discovered in 1810, over 180,000 seals were killed in three years and within ten years the herd was extinct (Ponting 1991: 183). Huge ocean tankers were built to transport the kills. This story was repeated incessantly everywhere on earth, until the early twentieth century when most animals now can live only in the most remote and isolated places. If we think that the earth has many animals today, imagine when they filled the skies, seas, prairies and forests!

There were attempts to resist the mass murder of animals throughout this period. By the early twentieth century a conservation ethic was sufficiently strong to make a plea to preserve the relatively few animals left. However by the time there was even a minimal ecological awakening, much of the damage had been done.

The current ecological movement has its roots in this history of conservation, preservation, and revulsion at the wanton destruction of life on earth.[4] Yet the association between men and their hunting rights runs deep. Efforts to stop or limit hunting in England and North America are met with fierce resistance. And the ecological movement is not consistent on its position. Even Aldo Leopold, the great trailblazer in ecophilosophy, feels that 'wildlife must be preserved, not because of the animals' inalienable right to life but rather because of man's inalienable right to hunt and kill' (Randall Eaton, *The Human/Animal Connection* [1985], quoted in Seager [1993]: 69). Male recreational hunting for pleasure or profit continues and animal extinctions are escalating at a staggering pace. In the words of feminist environmentalist Joni Seager: 'One cannot but be momentarily stunned by the enormous male population engaged in the destruction of wildlife, …these practices should be cause for declaration of an international emergency, … but is instead accepted as normal male behaviour' (Seager 1993: 213).

It is revealing to pause briefly on the associations between women and animals. Historically and still today in places, women are part of a man's

---

4.   The history of the ecological movement is very important in understanding how attitudes changed over time and how conservation came to be valued. For a good introduction to this history see Anna Bramwell, *Ecology in the 20th Century: A History* (1990).

property, including wives, daughters, goats, chickens and land. In addition to ownership of women and animals, the connection goes far. Ideologically both have been objectified, and are considered as 'game'. Men go on the hunt for 'a woman'. The words of Tennyson are illuminating: 'Man is the hunter; woman the game. The sleek shining creatures of the chase. Who hunts them for the beauty of their skins;/ They love us for it and we ride them down' (Seager 1993: 219). The connections with sexual assault are obvious. Violence against women often is animalized in language labelling women as meat, pussy, chicks, cows, etc. And finally, although the fur industry is often blamed on women, it is men who hunt, trap, kill, skin, auction, sell and buy furs, and reap the profits.

The pervasive domination of nature raises dozens of questions. How could such aggressive ideas and actions take hold so firmly and deeply in Euro-western consciousness? The domination of nature became not only the economic base and the means of progress, it became a worldview. To wreak havoc on the earth became so acceptable that those calling for conservation and preservation were labelled as ecoterrorists! Still today to stop cruelty to animals or to ask for animal rights or habitat preservation is too far out for mainstream culture. The cloning of animals is widely approved. The world of biotechnology is one further step towards the domination of life forms, this time at their genetic structures. To reconsider the genetic manipulation of animals and plants for food is interpreted by the dominant culture as opposing progress and wanting the 'third world' to starve!

The domination of the natural world has a long history. As well, this entire history cannot be understood only through an ecofeminist lens. Nonetheless, the previous conversations about the domination of women and the domination of nature do coalesce. To understand this final aspect in this quest for origins, it is necessary to take a look at the association of nature as female.

Nature as Female

There is an age-old history of imaging the earth or nature as female, be it as Mother Earth, Gaia, or various Goddesses. As far back as the origins of human culture, and virtually everywhere, there are remnants that indicate the earliest perceptions of the earth are as female. She represents the birthing of the universe or the earth, or as nurturing Mother Goddess. At times she symbolizes life itself and the whole earth as a sacred female reality. She is frequently imaged as an opulent woman. Fertility was understood as power belonging to the great cycles of birth and seasons. The ancient primordial Mother represents eternal creativity of the Earth and of women. Mother Nature represents an ancient and powerful tradition of associations between women and the natural world. It is found in figurines, cave paintings and burial practices that date back to early human settlements (Roach 2004). Thousands of images and stone replicas have been found throughout what is now Europe, the Middle East, Mexico, South America and elsewhere, dating back to 30,000 BCE.

In later periods, such as the times of classical cultures in Greece and Mesopotamia, there are myriad odes, hymns and prayers to the great Earth Goddesses, Mother Earth, or the Great Mother, such as this phrase from a Homeric hymn:

> The mother of us all, the oldest of all, hard, splendid as rock. Whatever there is that is of the land it is she who nourishes it.

Such images and writings are studied by feminists, and are often part of contemporary earth-based feminist spiritualities. What the proliferation of Mother/Goddess Earth relics and imagery means is uncertain. Did this imagery represent a time when the earth was considered to be sacred, and could not be reviled? Does this mean that women's fertility was connected to the mysteries of the Great Mother? The debate is intense. What is important here is to realize that there has been a long and venerable association between 'female' and nature that does not belong to any one culture or context. It has deep roots within human consciousness and spiritual sensitivities.

With the emergence of patriarchy and the decline of earth-based Goddesses, the natural world took on many diverse meanings. The Neolithic passage from hunter-gatherer and kin-based groupings to organized agriculture, priestly class and familial state systems took many centuries. With it came the erosion of the great Goddesses and the mythological transition to male Gods. Although remnants of the earth-based Goddesses and Mother Earth symbolism can be found throughout Euro-western civilization, there was a decided fermentation in the patriarchal intellectual traditions.

Since Euro-western traditions are heavily influenced by Greek rationalism, and many claim that classical Greece is the cradle of western civilization, ecofeminist Val Plumwood states that it is a useful place to start an examination of the human/nature, woman/nature dualisms (Plumwood 1993: 72).

In the eighth century BCE, Hesiod wrote of women as 'those with treachery in their hearts.' It was 'woman' who opened Pandora's box and scattered the evils upon the earth. Woman is responsible for the burdens and afflictions of men. He gives advice to men on how to deal with the problem of 'woman'. He writes, 'first purchase a house, a woman and a plow,' and then goes on to explain how to control her (O'Faolain and Martines, 1973: 4, 5).

In Sophocles' play *Antigone* (441 BCE) the chorus sang:

Oh earth is patient, and Earth is old
And a mother of Gods, but he breaketh her,
To-ing , froing, with the plough team going,
Tearing the soil of her, year by year.

The connections between sexual assault and agricultural practices are more than obvious.

The regulations surrounding women's lives were well established by the Homeric period of 1600 to 1100 BCE. Androcentrism and misogyny were the norm in the time of the founders of Euro-western civilization: Plato, Socrates and Aristotle. In their time the rulers had already established endless laws and customs for women, as well as class divisions. Although each contributed constructively to aspects of political organization, as well as in their metaphysical musings, their views of women and nature have been one of the sources of the women/nature nexus. By the time of Plato (approximately 428–348 BCE), the era of regarding the natural world as sacred, as an Earth or Mother Goddess, or even as saturated with numinous presence was being challenged. 'Nature' became the background of human culture. Philosophical questions turned towards ontology – the nature of being: of men, women, animals, and other aspects of earth life.

The power of logical thinking, rational categorizing, and the classifying of life became the predominant mode of knowing and relating to the world. The hierarchical–dualistic structure of Euro-western thought has its roots in a Greek form of rationality or reason that divided and differentiated the world into superior and inferior realms. The result was a division between the order of reason and the order of nature. The experience of life was divided along the dualisms that later became inherent in western rationalism. This fault line appears throughout the social structures, determining the 'nature of women' and that of men, which translates concretely into who can go out in public and at what time, who can be politically involved, what is of lower or higher nature, etc. While there is an overall appreciation of the cosmos or universe, the natural world was simply a setting for human endeavours. Although the worldview of the early Greek philosophers was not immediately influential, their writings offer the conceptual roots to the devaluation of both the natural and women. This onset of the negative associations of women and nature at the theoretical and symbolic levels are considered partially responsible for the current interlocking dominations of women and the earth.

The later Platonic period and up to the middle ages saw many variations in how Europeans viewed nature. For most of this period, the strong Greek devaluation of the earth was put aside. There is ample evidence to suggest that the earth was perceived as alive, animated, numinous or as an organism or vital organic whole. Ecofeminist Carolyn Merchant offers a plethora of examples over centuries that reveal the earth was believed to be alive or female (Merchant 1980). These beliefs functioned as ethical restraints on aggressive mining and deforestation, and were debated in politics, art and religion. For many, including influential religious thinkers such as Hildegard of Bingen and Thomas Aquinas, the earth and entire cosmos were alive with the presence of the Divine.

From the twelfth to the eighteenth century the European worldview changed dramatically. Christian interpretations of the world were losing credibility. As religious influence waned, Christianity opted for a disembodied and otherworldly spirituality creating a cultural space for an alternative view of the world. Philosophy and religion were in disagreement, and science as a new mode of knowing was rising. Galileo confirmed that the earth is not the centre of the universe. Christianity could not incorporate this new knowledge and began a fatal severing from science. Over a few hundred years the views of the earth changed. The earth, once alive was now dead and void of spirit. The earth was seen as mechanistic, as passive rather than active. The natural world was approached mathematically, establishing a desire to order and organize the earth, and to manage, master and control everything about the earth. The language of dissecting nature in order to force 'her' to reveal her secrets was common (Merchant 1980). The shift from an organistic to a mechanistic worldview is considered to be the beginning of the 'death of nature'.

Some individuals, such as Francis Bacon, one of the founders of science, were extremely influential in promoting a mechanistic worldview. For example he wrote:

> Man, if we look to final causes, may be regarded as the center of the world, insomuch that if man were taken away from the world, the rest would seem to be all astray, without aim or purpose … Let the human race recover that right over Nature which belongs to it by divine bequest. (quoted in Ponting 1991: 148)

In another instance Bacon wrote:

> We can, if need be, ransack the whole globe, penetrate into the bowels of the earth, descend to the bottom of the deep, travel to the farthest regions of this world to acquire wealth, to increase out knowledge, or even only to please out eye and fancy. (quoted in Merchant, 1980: 249)

Nature was not only seen in mechanistic terms, but also in misogynist ones. Bacon combined the mastery over nature with sexual domination. He wrote of 'entering and penetrating into the holes and corners'; that nature must be bound into service, and made a slave, that nature must be taken by the forelock and captured, and forced out of her natural state, squeezed and molded. In short nature is to be raped (Merchant, 1980: 169–70).

The masculine, mechanistic and misogynist worldview took hold. It fostered the predominant mode of combative interaction with the natural world. Although there was always opposition and dissenting voices, a mechanistic approach overtook ethics of stewardship or conservation, and beliefs of earth's animism or vitality. Because this mechanistic worldview or belief system was accepted as true, the fact that it was and is extremely ecologically predacious has been all but ignored.

The mechanistic worldview reunited with the hierarchical dualisms mentioned at the beginning of this chapter. In addition to the dualisms mentioned before (superior/inferior, reason/emotion, mind/body, culture/nature, heaven/earth, spirit/matter, divine/demonic and man/woman), the mechanistic worldview added more:

reason	nature
human	nature(non-human)
rationality	animality (irrational)
public	private
subject	object
logic	chaos
production	reproduction
power	powerless
father(male)	others
civilized	primitive (savage, animal)
enlightened	unenlightened
master	slave
universal	particular

These dualisms, when combined together, reveal and reflect forms of domination that permeate and structure Euro-western societies. Colonization, slavery, misogyny, ethnocentrism, andro- and anthropocentrism, and the disregard for the natural world are all pieces of this worldview. According to ecofeminist Val Plumwood, these forms of domination 'accumulated a store of such conceptual weapons, which can be mined, refined and redeployed for new uses' (Plumwood 1993: 43).

These, coupled with a revolutionary idea of progress and economic growth, solidified into beliefs, social structures and organizational principles. The emerging emphasis on economic development paved the way for industrial capitalism, whereby the earth could be 'mined' or 'raped' for all its benefits, including the most recent form of economic globalization. This period of history has resulted in rapacious extractions from the natural world and an ecological crisis of unprecedented proportions. The fifteenth and sixteenth centuries saw the rise of a European world economy that excluded women and nature from its consideration except where it found an opportunity to exploit them. The accumulation of capital was essential in order for 'the capitalist mode of production [to] establish and maintain itself' (Mies 1986: 88), and 'most of this capital was not accumulated through "honest" trade by merchant capitalists but largely by way of brigandage, piracy, forced and slave labour' (Mies 1986: 89). The rise of mechanistic science and economic 'progress' coincides with the accelerating butchery of animals.

The scientific, mechanistic, capitalist worldview took over Euro-western cultures, and continues to dominate today. Hierarchical dualisms seem to skulk in the shadows of our understanding and organization of the world, and rear their heads only when challenged with alternative ways to appreciate and order things. Ecofeminists have probed this process at length, and comprehend how systems of domination are derived from such dualisms.

Women, Nature, and the Natural World: The Theoretical Cluster

Ecofeminists study the question of the origins of domination, both of women and of the natural world and the two combined. These factors, data and theories are put together into a cluster of analyses that sheds some light on the quest for origins. The origins of domination are enigmatic, but are known to involve patriarchy, androcentrism and anthropocentrism in an enmeshed history of ideas and events. There is much more involved than can be discussed here, but it gives a taste of how ecofeminists assess the historical roots and possible sources of the current problems. There is an undeniable connection between women and the natural world in Euro-western societies. Their mutual dominations are clearly symbolically and materially associated.

As described, it is important to bear in mind that in addition to their affiliated subjugation, both women and nature are assaulted for additional reasons that are not related to each other. The feminizing of nature and the naturalizing of women are only one aspect of their domination. To reduce the ecological crisis and the oppression of women to even the most substantial ecofeminist critique would be mistaken. Women are dominated just for being women. The natural world is dominated often due to fear and the desire for mastery and control. Both may be dominated simply because they can be, and because power is seductive and control gives a sense of superiority in a world of vulnerability and death.

Domination has been studied by many kinds of analysis and from several angles. What has been discovered is that domination in any form seems to share certain characteristics. Ecofeminist Val Plumwood, for example, outlines similar features among all ideologies of domination. Such ideologies are based on categories of difference and exclusion, within which the hierarchical dualisms are operative (Plumwood 1995: 12–13). She describes five characteristics of all domination as: (1) *Radical exclusion*; the 'other' is both inferior and radically separate. Women possess a different nature, the natural world is ontologically other, and both are subordinated allowing for a dominant identity to be established against the subordinated identities. This justifies controlling privileges, and access to goods and limiting the power of the inferior groups. (2) *Homogenization*; differences and diversity within the otherness is disregarded, and domination appears to be natural. (3) *Denial or backgrounding*; that woman and natural world are unessential or act as a background to the significant activities. Backgrounding denies the dependency on the other, but allows the dominator to make use of, organize, rely on and benefit from the other's services – yet repudiate the other's contribution or even existence. Slaves exist only in the background to the dominant group. (4) *Incorporation*; identifying the other in relation to the man as central. Men's features are universalized, and women, 'others' and the natural world are exceptions, and inferior. (5) *Instrumentalism*; social worth is derived instrumentally, according to the desires of the dominating protector.

This analysis offers a framework to help identify the elements within systems of domination, one in which ecofeminists situate the domination of nature. Rather than accentuate one form of domination, or simply continually list the dominating 'isms,' the substructure provides a useful analytic tool. For Plumwood, all domination is rooted in a common ideology based on the control of reason over nature. What each oppressed group shares is their ideological association with the sphere of nature (Plumwood 1993: 74). Ecofeminists see domination as a core phenomenon at the ideological and material roots of the women/nature nexus.

Questions about Origins

The Force of Ideas

There is much debate in the quest for origins about the actual influence of ideas in historical development. At times ideas shape the world, and at others the material realities or events shape the ideas. This dialectic is neither clear-cut nor static. Events, such as the Black Death wherein one third of Europe was dead within a few decades, shaped a worldview that feared and despised 'nature' (Herlihy 1997). Conceivably such an overwhelming physical and psychic shock was a precursor to the extreme forms of the domination of nature. This bleak period was also accompanied and followed by the Inquisition, whereby thousands of women were murdered as witches, because they were closer to 'nature' than men, and nature was the realm of the demonic.

The long history of the emergence of domination is complex. It involves the rise of patriarchy and androcentrism, the domestication and destruction of the natural world, the oppression of women, and the merging of the natural world as female into a large cluster of suppositions, theories and practices.

Certainly one can point to the history of hierarchical dualisms as evidence of a thread throughout this time. There is sufficient historical testimony that in the realm of ideas about the world, they were present and prevalent. It is also obvious that they validated and justified the oppression of women and an escalating plundering of the natural world. However ecofeminists who assert that the current crisis has *solid* foundations in this history of hierarchical dualisms may be stretching the claim, for three reasons. First, although the coherence of hierarchical dualisms is self evident, this must not be confused with a direct coherence throughout history. The cause and effect of the dualisms is difficult to determine, and it is neither a historically linear nor a socially logical progression. Second, although these dualisms were operative, and certainly used to dominate, both women and nature were never 'only' what was designated them by the hegemonic ideological framework (Sandilands 1999: 19). The social location of women, the complexity of ecosystems, and the changing socio-political landscapes defy being categorized neatly into these dualistic structures. As well, although the philosophical and theological currents imposed their idealized and negative categories on women, how far women themselves identified with this construct of 'woman' is not really known. It is certain that some women opposed it, and for centuries. Third, it is very difficult to determine how embedded these ideas became in Euro-western development, and how far they are responsible for the ecological crisis and concurrent domination of women. That they are culpable is undeniable. The question is to what extent? Even today these same hierarchical dualisms continue to feel familiar. It is surprising to find in teaching that, year after year, students are able to make the lists of dualisms without ever having consciously thought of them before. It must be recognized that the internalized learning and patterns of hierarchical domination are deeply programmed. Are these dualisms still shaping Euro-western cultures, and resulting in ecological suicide and rampant misogyny? Yes, and no.

Historical processes are neither unified nor homogenous. Although histories are told as coherent narratives, that is not how they were lived. Many contradictory practices and ideas co-exist, competing for public, political and ideological space, influencing and being influenced by their specific context. Events take on a life of their own, and then shape the ideas. It is crucial to appreciate the dynamism and dialectic between ideas, events and materiality. A monolithic view of these dualisms presents an extremely limited and inaccurate view of history. Nonetheless they are consistently present and influential throughout the uneven path of Euro-western societies.

Conclusion

Domination has a long and intricate historical path. The origins are buried in both an enigmatic past and within the recesses of human consciousness. Yet in spite of the uncertainties, such research is invaluable. This theoretical work does three things. First it brings to consciousness the history, as the past is important to understand the present. Second it makes us aware of the implicit values hidden in worldviews. Without an awareness of our worldviews we believe them to be true without ever having questioned their validity. Third, to understand patriarchy, domination, misogyny and the oppression of the natural world, and especially their interconnections, is to open the possibility of dismantling it by denunciation. What is relevant today is that ecofeminism challenges patriarchy on moral and spiritual grounds, and insists that regardless of its origins, the era and pertinence of patriarchy is over.

To understand these issues even a little is also to create a space for alternatives to be imaged. As yet there is no alternative paradigm immediately available to take its place. Still there are colossal amounts of energy being poured into developing new theoretical frameworks, imagining original patterns of relationships based on mutuality rather than hierarchy, discovering ingenious methods of resistance and sabotage, and creating new forms of living.

Religions have a lot to learn with respect to their own women/nature nexus. Religious histories need to be probed on the questions raised in this chapter. Religions and religious insights are powerful influences in human affairs, in spite of their ambiguous ideas and effects. Theologians have learned a great deal from ecofeminism, and are contributors to its development. Some are deeply engaged in this cultural deconstruction and reconstruction. The next chapter moves into the specific areas of ecofeminism and theology.

Chapter Three

The Ecological Crisis and Religion: Ecofeminist Theology

Ecofeminism is about the mutual domination and liberation of women and the natural world. It is a broad intersection with many routes and directions. The quest for origins reveals an uneven, indefinite and camouflaged past. Ecofeminists claim there is sufficient evidence that women and the natural world are interlaced in a complex synthesis of hierarchical dualisms embedded in a patriarchal worldview and social structures. This claim is one of the bases for ecofeminist theology, because Christianity has been one of the chief proponents of this worldview.

Christianity: Women, Nature and Patriarchal Problems

An early link between ecofeminism and theology was within the feminist critical analyses of the Euro-western cultural history and heritage. The theoretical and theological ideals and presuppositions were studied to discover the determining roots of misogyny and the domination of the earth.[1] It was evident that the Jewish and Christian traditions were implicated in fostering the dual oppressions of women and 'nature'. Such work has been foundational to further ecofeminist study.

---

1. Rosemary Radford Ruether has contributed to such analysis: *New Woman/New Earth* (1975); *Sexism and God Talk: Towards a Feminist Theology* (1983); *Gaia & God: An Ecofeminist Theology of Earth Healing* (1992). In a similar vein is the work of Elizabeth Dobson Gray, *Patriarchy as a Conceptual Trap* (1984). Susan Griffin's brilliant work, *Women and Nature: The Roaring Inside Her* (1978), offers historical streams of thought on women and the earth, indicating the formation of Euro-western cultures as based on these dual dominations. Further, ecofeminist thought is interdisciplinary, drawing from feminist research in history, social analysis, philosophy, and recently science.

The role of Christianity in the dual subjugation of women and the natural world is evident, yet not straightforward. Christianity is many things. The institution with its history of texts and tomes is only one form of its cultural presence. How Christianity was and is lived is extremely difficult to assess, as the variants are vast. Christianity has never been homogenous. It has its roots firmly planted within diverse elements of Judaism yet is deeply shaped by Greek philosophy and by European history. It has rambled and lumbered through history and cultures, uniting with and dividing from the state, making absolute claims and then refuting them. It has influenced virtually all aspects of culture and social life from grandiose claims about the cosmos to directives about the intimate details of living. At times, and in some places, Christianity was a liberating movement on the social and political fringes, and a voice for freedom and justice. At other times it was in bed with the dominant and destructive powers of the day. At times the liberation and justice movements were against the churches, and at times with. Or it was both, at the same time and place! Christianity has been able to mediate a sacred presence, and at times obscure it. In the end Christianity is not something 'out there', but rather it is what communities, cultures, and people have made of it. Christianity is really an amalgamation of many influences and represents an endless variety of sub-traditions lived in an endless variety of cultural contexts. From this vantage point Christianity is an enormously complicated, historically cumbersome, contradictory, and indeed both a liberatory and oppressive social and religious reality.

History never discloses the complexities of its time. Recorded history is most often the narrative of the victors, the literate, the powerful and the ruling group. The underside of history is not usually recorded, or can only be found from reading 'between the lines'. Some Christian teachings did not reflect the reality of what was occurring in the society, but rather what they wanted to occur. Some classic Christian tomes represented only the views of that individual. Much of what is studied in the 'history of Christianity' is about debates among clerics on their views on a vast array of topics. What everyone else lived within and outside of the parameters of Christianity is not well known. There are only fragments offering glimpses of women's realities (Malone 2001, 2002, 2003). As always, life is more complex and uneven than can be manifested in texts or records. Even with seemingly endless instructions to and edicts about women, it is difficult to assess how, and how much, they were lived out. As well, for every view within the tradition there was a counter-one, even if a minority view. While the leaders proclaimed the inferior nature of women, others would take the same reasons or biblical references to claim the opposite. On other occasions women and men of good will would use elements of the bible or tradition to advance the status of women to liberate them from social limits. At times women were romanticized and sentimentalized for their virtues, and at other times vilified for their moral weakness.

The Women/Nature Nexus

To read Christian history and writings through an ecofeminist lens reveals that women and the natural world were, at times, the topics of much debate. To claim that Christianity is the source of the domination of women, or of the natural world, or of both together, is too simplistic. Yet it is undeniable that Christianity has played a role, perhaps even as a key player, in these dominations. The following examples will indicate that the oppression of women, the negation and domination of the natural world, and at times the two together, have been a piece of the Christian fabric. While I am not minimizing the detrimental influences of these elements of Christian worldviews and practices, I am cautioning against a direct interpretation of cause and effect within enormously varied, convoluted and perplexing historical processes.

Anyone who has even briefly examined Christianity – the bible, the earliest texts and records, the endless statements, and the historical practices – cannot deny that many influential Christian leaders were not generous in their attitudes and actions towards women. Of course there were other voices, and Christianity is not synonymous with the oppression of women. As well, today feminists find many resources within the tradition and in contemporary interpretations. For the moment, however, I am emphasizing those teachings that reveal a misogynist and anti-nature stance within Christianity.

In terms of the bible, it is full of views about women, and many women are nameless. There are frequent comparisons between what constitutes the good or the bad woman. Women are either. This is readily seen in the differences between Eve and Mary, the adulterous/sexual woman or the virtuous wife, the disobedient or obedient woman, the unfaithful harlot or the woman faithful to Israel/Yahweh, the barren worthless woman or the fecund wife, and the ultimate image of the virgin mother. Many women in the bible are discussed as belonging to this or that man, or are owned by men. Daughters and extra wives are considered to be property, given away as dowry, or as concubines to men; they are offered to be raped as a gesture of 'hospitality'. Wives are returned to brothers, fathers or uncles if they are widowed. Androcentrism is blatant and misogyny is not hard to find. Of course, it was not considered misogyny at the time because it was simply the way things were. There are images and stories of women who are valiant, who refuse to accept their lot in life, and who are liberating images for women. There are liberating motifs throughout the bible, such as justice, freedom, preferential options for the poor and female wisdom figures. The person and teachings of Jesus have been studied and interpreted to be constructive for women, and Jesus is understood by some to have been less patriarchal than his peers and culture.

In places where Christianity was not the source but rather absorbed intense anti-women views, spokesmen of the tradition seemed to do little to refute them. Later, and once Christianity established itself as the state political and religion system, they initiated anti-women ideas and practices. From the earliest times to the present, the Christian religion, as a social, political and historical force, has been deeply patriarchal, with all that it entails. Because the bible is still considered to be a sacred text, and is predominantly patriarchal, it gives patriarchy a sacred blessing.

Overtime Christianity absorbed and developed the hierarchical dualisms described in Chapter Two. In Christian teachings women became affiliated with nature and both were considered to be inherently corrupt. For example, Tertullian taught that the women are the devil's gateway, and are the cause of 'man's' corruption, that the devil enters the world through women, and women are closer to the earth than men.[2] Women were blamed for bringing sin into the world. Eve was used as the exemplar of 'woman' and sin, as her nature was corrupt and needed redeeming. Women have been constantly blamed for being seductive, or so beautiful that men, against their will, are drawn into sin. Women have been understood to be the property of a man, and thus cannot be seen to be desirable in the eyes of other men. It is the fault of the woman if other men desire her. In some cultures women are killed for even a hint of sexual transgression, such as flirting. If a young woman is raped, she may be murdered by her kin for staining the family honour. Male members of a family believe they can only regain their family honour by murdering females for alleged sexual transgressions. These are known as 'honour killings'. They exist in many countries today.

There are regulations in many religions for women being partially or fully covered. Clement of Alexandria wrote: 'By no means are women to be allowed to uncover and exhibit any part of their person' (Roberts and Donaldson 1867: 209).

For centuries many Christian leaders taught that men were spiritual and women were bodily; that men, not women, were in the image of God; that women were born of nature and men were born of spirit; that women were intellectually like children and needed to be controlled; and that both nature

---

2.   See Tertullian, *Des Cultu Feminarim*, quoted in Julia O'Faolain and Lauro Martines (eds.), *Not in God's Image: Women in History from the Greeks to the Victorians* (1973: 13–33).

and women had inherent chaotic forces and must be controlled. In the later middle ages, church law was becoming systematic. 'Law' as such was a mixture of Christian beliefs, patriarchal power and religious control. What is considered to be legal is often simply the reflection of the biases of the worldview. For example, a legal excerpt from the year 1140 reads:

> Women should be subject to their men. The natural order for mankind is that women should serve men, and children their parents, for it is just that the lesser serve the greater. The image of God is in man. ... Therefore woman is not made in God's image. Woman's authority is nil; let her in all things be subject to man'.
> (O'Faolain and Martines 1973: 130)

Prominent Christian theologians and philosophers from the time of Augustine, Tertullian, and Jerome to almost the twentieth century decided that nature was chaotic and unruly, and because women were closer to nature, therefore women were the same. Both had to be constrained by men. Educating women was unnatural, and indeed useless. Women were disdained for being too emotional, intellectually feeble, spiritually soiled and able to corrupt men. Women, as virgins, were less tainted. Virgin mothers were the best; although a goal hard to attain!

A notable, and deplorable, description of these kinds of teachings is found in *Malleus Maleficarum*, or the Witch Hammer, written in 1486 by Heinrich Kramer and James Sprenger. It is one of the most misogynist Christian texts ever written. It was created during the Inquisition, and was to aid the identification, prosecution, and murdering of women as witches. It brought into focus the worst of Christian views about women and nature. It placed into the Christian imagination and consciousness a belief that non-virtuous women and witches are a threat to the Christian world; a belief still held in places today. Estimates of the death toll during the Inquisition range from 600,000 to as high as several millions (over 250 years); nearly all of the accused were women.

Historically, and for many centuries, Christianity was predominantly an urban phenomenon. It was about beliefs, complex social structures and intellectual ideals and ideas. The Christian movement throughout Europe did not affect nor was interested in the pagan or country dwellers. Early Christianity was not addressing those who lived on farms or in small rural communities, or whose livelihood and worldview were derived from the land. Later these country dwellers were deemed to be inferior to those in urban settings, and the term pagan was reinterpreted to mean non-believers or those who held superstitious beliefs. In this way an anti-nature bias was endemic to some extent.

In the middle ages and beyond, nature was approached mathematically. God was the great clock-maker, ordering the world. The natural world was dead, void of spirit, even corrupt. It took men away from God. Nature was not the realm of the drama of salvation, or was a deterrent. Salvation and redemption were interpreted as rising above nature. The corrupt 'nature' of the natural world was seen as inseparable from the same corrupt 'nature' of women. Both were then rejected as being inferior to men and God. The worst of these teachings claimed that the earth was perceived to be irrelevant to God or even demonic, and women and nature were to serve men and God. These and similar proclamations were an integral part of Christian teachings (Griffin 1978).

Christianity is also many other things. Some women throughout the centuries have experienced the tradition as affirming, liberatory and truth-giving. And there have always been Christians who experience the Divine in the natural world. One does not negate the other. However, theologians who engage with ecofeminism must come to terms with both of these realities; the degrading legacy and the liberatory potential.

The impact of this negative heritage of Christianity has not yet been fully realized. Christianity has deeply influenced Euro-western cultural beliefs and practices. It is futile to study the ecological crisis and the problems of women in Euro-western cultures without appreciating the impact and repercussions of these aspects of Christian worldviews. While most contemporary cultures continue to be patriarchal, and exhibit at least some of the hierarchical dualisms, there are specific influences in each culture. In Euro-western contexts the predominant religious influence is Christianity. Whether one considers oneself or the particular country Christian, the consequences of the Christian tradition are forceful, and cannot be bypassed.

Christianity and the Ecological Crisis

The ecological crisis is creating a new context for theology. Some theologians have not yet recognized this while others are uncertain whether the existing theological systems can respond. It is crucial to grasp that the ecological crisis cannot simply be added to the current problems and religious reflections. The prevailing frameworks are not adequate. The same can be said of feminism, in that women's concerns cannot simply be added to 'religion'. The challenge of feminism to Christianity has been massive. The challenge of ecofeminism is even greater.

What is also important to realize is that an ecological crisis of this magnitude, and with such enigmatic causes within human ideologies and worldviews, has never existed previously. The biblical and Christian traditions, or other religions for that matter, are not equipped to respond to such a crisis. They did not arise from, nor address in any depth, ecological issues. To expect abundant ecological resources from religions in their current form is mistaken. However, all world religions deal with the interrelations between humans, the natural world and the Divine, and all influence ecological practices. They have direct and indirect resources, such as prophetic voices, claims for justice, notions of revelation, rituals, symbols, and languages of the Sacred that could be oriented towards ecological sustainability. In some traditions, especially Indigenous spiritualities from around the world, the earth is experienced as Sacred and revelatory. It is these resources and experiences that are immensely needed today. Religious traditions also have abundant resources in their buildings and land, and can communicate weekly or even daily with the millions of peoples who attend temples, synagogues and churches. As well, religions represent the *only* institutions in the world that have an intricate network of grassroots, national and international structures virtually everywhere. Quite a set of resources!

The Ecological Challenge to Theology

Theology, Truth Claims and Transparency
For centuries the main dialogue partner for theology was philosophy, notably metaphysics. Since the 1960s there has been a shift to dialoguing with the social sciences: social and critical theories of liberation, economics, cultural studies and political sciences. This has fostered a host of new views and new theologies. Feminist theology required the use of multi-disciplinary feminist theories, which led to an additional partner in epistemology. Epistemology is that field of study that asks about the business of 'knowing' anything. It asks how we know what we know, how much can we really know, how religions make truth claims, and what kind of truth. Feminist theology began asking a long list of questions about all these proclamations about women, and on what bases was this 'known'. Theology has also expanded by using postcolonial analyses, postmodern evaluations of meta-narratives, context and culture-specific insights, and feminist economics. The result has been a vast array of items that fall under the term 'theology'. With the necessary distinctions among denominational differences, cultural context, social location, ethnic origin, dialogue partner, sexual orientation and author-interests, theology is really an umbrella term for 'theologies'.

Religions are not always transparent about how they make their claims. What kind of truth is proclaimed? What are the sources? How are they used?

From what perspectives is theology done? By and for whom? In whose interests? And to what ends? Most progressive contemporary theologies try to be transparent about these issues. Although a daring generalization, theologies that are not transparent about these distinctions are more likely to make claims of universal objective truths while really operating from patriarchal, white, colonial and heterosexist systems of power and privilege. This may become clearer with an illustration from feminist theology. For example, the Christian tradition claims that all humans are equal and in the image of God, while at the same time has denied, and continues to deny in some places, half of humanity full freedom to express this image. The excessive male language for God and humanity is known to be detrimental to women, and reinforces male power over women. Yet the Christian tradition as a whole worldwide resists inclusive language for God, even though doctrinally God is beyond gender. The patriarchs will unabashedly say, 'God is not male, *He* is love'! However the connections are not made between the religious teachings, the power systems and the social consequences. In the confrontation between patriarchal and feminist theologies, theology has been forced into a self-scrutiny on the relationships between theological claims and historical, socio-political, economic and gender consequences. Yet, such scrutiny has not happened consistently, uniformly, or readily, and continues to be met with resistance in places.

The ecological crisis demands a further transparency and a more radical critique of theology. It requires in-depth awareness of the ecological outcomes of religious claims. It demands bringing all resources to bear to mitigate ecological ruin, even if that means revisioning and reconstructing elements within the traditions. It also means coming to terms with how religious worldviews function. In addition, for religions to adequately address the ecological crisis, the dialogue partners must be further enlarged to include the earth sciences. The first steps in addressing the ecological crisis and its relationship to theology is to ask these questions about truth, assumptions, dialogue partners and transparancy. If the next step is to move to ecofeminist theology, then it is important to first discuss the larger field of ecological-theology (ecotheology).

Ecotheology and Questions about Method

Ecotheology stands for all the work that brings together ecological and theological views. Although ecotheology is a recent term, a few have been insisting for decades that theologians examine ecological concerns.[3] Today it is still less than ten per cent of theologians or those in religious studies who consider

---

3.   John Cobb has been concerned about ecological problems for over twenty years. See *Foundations* 17.2 (1974). See also the works of Thomas Berry (1988; 1999).

ecological realities in their work, or mention them only in passing.[4] Yet as Jürgen Moltmann aptly stated in 1985:

> Our situation today is determined by the ecological crisis of our whole scientific and technological civilization, and by the exhaustion of nature through human beings. This crisis is deadly. …Unless there is a radical reversal in the fundamental orientation of our human societies, and unless we succeed in finding an alternative way of living and dealing with other living things and with nature, this crisis is going to end in a wholesale catastrophe. (Moltmann 1985: 20)

There is an endless amount of topics to cover between ecology and theology. Even to present the history of Christian notions of the natural world and the ambiguous relationship between Christian theology, the natural world and the ecological crisis would require a few books! Usually a first step is to examine the criticism that the Christian tradition is partially responsible for ecological destruction.

The ecological dangers of Christianity were noticed in the late 1960s by several people, including Alan Watts (1958), Lynn White (1967), Gregory Bateson (1972), and Arnold Toynbee (1974). They, for different reasons, warned that the particular Christian worldview of Euro-western cultures is ecologically destructive.[5] At the beginning of ecotheology, these accusations were debated. By 1985 it was generally accepted that while Christianity is not solely to blame for propelling Christian cultures towards ecological ruin, there are elements within the tradition that are seen as ignoring or even promoting detrimental human–earth relations (Santmire 1985: 1–29). As James Nash writes: 'the central thrust of the ecological complaint against Christianity therefore should not be discounted. Christianity has done too little to discourage, and too much to encourage the exploitation of nature' (Nash 1991: 74). Thus, by 1990 or so, ecological complaint against Christianity, while not self-evident, was generally accepted as having some validity.

There are numerous *methods* within ecotheology. The term method refers to the approaches, types of questions, tools for analysis, and notions of truth in

---

4.   One simply has to examine the books, conferences, statements and rituals – of which there are thousands daily, or more, around the world – to be convinced that there are few who say the ecological crisis is a central religious concern. Ten per cent is generous!

5.   Watts argued that Christianity is an urban religion that fits poorly with nature and has encouraged technological transformations of the natural world. Toynbee found that the monotheism supplanted a nature-reverencing pantheism and desacralized nature. White blamed Christianity as being 'the most anthropocentric religion the world has seen', quoted in Nash, *Loving Nature* (1990: 69–70).

any given inquiry. Theological methods add further questions about presuppositions or assumptions about religion, the world, and ultimately the worldview. Theological method is an enormous field of study!

There are at least five distinct methods of associating theology and ecology. Such 'methods' involve numerous worldview and religious assumptions. The first one involves disagreeing that there are connections to Christianity, and to dispute the ecological complaint against Christianity (Nash 1991: 68–92). One may realize the severity of the ecological crisis and the need for immediate action, but it is not related to religion. Or it may mean that the ecological crisis is irrelevant, because Christian revelation is not about earth-life and relates only to human salvation, especially after death. A second method is based on a belief that the devastation of the earth is part of the biblical apocalyptic predictions, and therefore it is a good sign that the end is near. It is an infrequent interpretation, but nonetheless there.[6] A third method comes from those who consider the Christian system to be ecologically bankrupt (Santmire 1985: 1).[7] They have turned elsewhere, such as to eastern, Goddess or Indigenous traditions or new age spiritualities, in order to find spiritual and theological resources.

Most ecotheology begins with the fourth and fifth methods, those that constructively connect ecology and Christianity. The fourth could be called an apologetic approach. The purpose is to re-examine the tradition for ignored ecological sensitivities, or to reorient the familiar and basic tenets in light of the ecological crisis. Such ecotheologians highlight ecological sensitivities within texts and the tradition. They point to influential Christians who manifested an awareness of the earth, such as Hildegard of Bingen or Francis of Assisi. They engage in ecological reinterpretations of principal Christian themes such as the Covenant, Spirit, Incarnation, love of neighbour and a renewed understanding of creation. Many offer alternative ecological interpretations of scripture, doctrine and liturgy.[8] The union between ecology and justice –

---

6. This interpretation is not only within Christianity. In a conversation with a learned Daoist friend, when I expressed my distress over the ecological crisis he asked why I would even try to resist it as that would be going against the Dao.

7. Santmire does not advocate this, but rather sees Christianity as ambiguous in its relationship to an ecological framework.

8. I would include such work as the stewardship approach by Douglas Hall, *The Steward: A Biblical Symbol Come of Age* (1990); systematic approaches by Moltmann, *God in Creation* (1985); works by Leonardo Boff, *Ecology and Liberation: A New Paradigm* (1995); Sean McDonagh, *Passion for the Earth: The Christian Vocation to Promote Justice, Peace and Integrity of Creation* (1994); David Hallman (ed.), *Ecotheology: Voices from South and North* (1993); Dieter Hessel (ed.), *After Nature's Revolt: Eco-Justice and Theology* (1992); Charles Birch, William Eakin and Jay McDaniel (eds.), *Liberating Life: Contemporary Approaches to Ecological Theology* (1990); Jay McDaniel, *Earth, Sky, Gods, and Mortals: Developing an*

ecojustice – is prevalent here. This search for and interpretation of resources within the tradition is ongoing. At times the emphasis seems to be on making Christianity environmentally friendly rather than on mitigating ecological ruin. Nonetheless an apologetic approach is both valid and necessary, and is the most prevalent among ecotheological responses. Finally, a fifth method is to engage in a radical revisioning of an understanding of religion and religious truths. It seeks to reawaken a sense of the sacredness of the earth using multiple avenues and options, including within Christianity. The dialogue partners are numerous, including science, feminism, postmodernism, cosmology, inter-religious insights and spirituality. Their primary goal is to rekindle a religious experience of the earth and to resist further ecological degradation. They validate the sacred dimension to the earth community, use all resources available, and are reworking a deepened understanding of religion in general and Christianity in particular. In general ecofeminists use the latter two methods.

Ecofeminist Theology and Methods
Ecofeminist theology is beginning to reshape aspects of the Christian tradition. Prior to ecofeminism, the ecological crisis and feminist analyses were independently influencing theological reflections. Given that each is profoundly challenging to mainstream religious traditions, it would follow that ecofeminism is a combination of both of these challenges. Also, ecofeminism is often more radical than other voices in ecotheology because it has already rejected hierarchical dualisms, and is accustomed to a deep probing of assumptions and methods of analysis. This means that when ecofeminism contacts theology, there are no facile rearrangements, and no straightforward solutions to developing ecofeminist theologies. One of the most difficult aspects is that when ecofeminism encounters theology, core issues are raised.

Core issues can be described in terms of a question: How far must theology be reshaped to adequately address ecological and feminist concerns? There is a great difference between seeing the ecological crisis as an addendum to the list of Christian concerns and re-examining the fundamental human–earth–Divine relationships. For now I want to accentuate this difference, albeit it is artificial at times. If the ecological crisis is to be simply added to the theological radar screen, the work is to incorporate and interpret ecological concerns within the existing theological systems. Here the primary context is the religious system. Responses tend to be in the form of reinterpretations of theological doctrines or motifs. Using such an approach one may seek biblical references that,

Ecological Spirituality (1990); James Conlon, *Geo-Justice: A Preferential Option for the Earth* (1990); and McFague, *The Body of God* (1993)

for example, negate ecological destruction and promote responsibility. Stewardship and ecojustice are the predominant expressions of this form of approach.[9] One can reread scriptures, traditions, themes of creation, Cosmic Christ, justice for all and preferential option for the poor and add the earth crisis into these themes. In all cases the ecological crisis is brought into the Christian worldview, the starting and ending point is the tradition. The religious framework is not fundamentally altered. This is a tradition-centred approach.

The second way pursues a more radical reconstruction that seeks to include the theological system (religious tradition) within the earth context, or an earth-centred approach. It involves a rethinking of the entire perspective from which one does theology. The starting point is the earth, and thus the four billion year evolution of the earth. To be earth-centred opens the possibility of considering the earth and its evolution as the elemental and primary realm of revelation. All life, including the rich complexities of human civilizations and religions, are seen as emergent from these great earth processes. Human animals with their two million year history represent a very recent moment of earth history. Religion and human civilizations have between a ten and twenty thousand year history. Thus, religions arose quite recently from within this great history, and there have been a multitude of religious experiences and traditions as well as spiritual sensitivities. Within this multiplicity, Christianity is only one expression of religious awareness and spiritual consciousness. Thus religions cannot be the primary reference points for the whole earth, but rather specific religions may be a primary reference point for some human communities grappling with their existence.

An earth-centred approach is incompatible with a tradition-centred one. This means that in an earth-centred approach, the earth is primary; no life and no religious tradition can flourish without earth health. A tradition-centred approach means that the tradition and all that it stands for has primacy. Human life and religions are the main reference and starting point. An earth-centred approach means that the earth and its traditions and history have primacy, and are the reference and starting point. It is about which of these has ultimate

9. More will be said about ecojustice as justice as a crucial component of the approach to the alliance between cosmology and ecofeminism. What I am delineating at present is a position that would contend that if justice is a central Christian motif, then justice to the earth is not only the rallying call but is the most relevant and viable theological method. Justice as such, while deemed imperative, does not address the extreme anthropocentrism implicit throughout the hegemonic theological assumptions. Therefore a theological methodology *centred* on justice is considered necessary but insufficient.

priority. For example, in both instances the bible is relevant. In a tradition-centred approach we would look for inspiration within biblical texts, seek ecologically oriented texts, interpret and stretch the message of Jesus to include the earth, expand justice to ecojustice, etc. But in an earth-centred approach the earth is a primary source of inspiration, as the earth is the source of humans and human consciousness. The bible is understood as one sacred text among many within the long journey towards a consciousness of the Sacred. From an earth-centred view, religious texts are part of the recording of a deep spiritual awakening within human consciousness at a stage in human history when social organization was sufficiently developed. These texts, in turn, are expressions of human experiences of living in, and being an integral part of, a divine milieu. Revelations have many forms, and spiritual consciousness is not limited to any one understanding. From here we can see that the theological challenge is immense, and core issues are central. This is echoed by Rasmussen who states that 'our whole way of thinking must be restructured, ...the ecocrisis is a foundational challenge' (Rasmussen 1994: 173).

Ecofeminist Theology

People come to ecofeminism through a variety of paths, as illustrated in Chapter One. Theologians can take any number of these paths. Some wade through the historical morass of the Christian views of women and nature. Others add ecological concerns to their social and/or feminist critiques and commitments. Some become so alarmed by the ecological crisis they move towards ecofeminism seeking assistance. The entry points differ, and the range and depth of ecological and feminist analyses vary extremely. Ecofeminist theology is to be understood as a loose term denoting the contributions that join together ecology, theology and feminism. As feminist theologies engage further with ecological concerns, and as ecofeminist analyses mature and become a dialogue partner with both feminist and ecological theologies, we can begin to speak of ecofeminist theologies (Eaton 1996).

Ecofeminism and theology/religion have explicitly intersected for two decades, initiated by Rosemary Radford Ruether's *New Woman, New Earth* (1975). Further reflection has moved the conversation in numerous directions. Elizabeth Johnson summarizes the basic idea:

> I am persuaded by the truth of the ecofeminist insight that analysis of the ecological crisis does not get to the heart of the matter until it sees the connection between the exploitation of the earth and the sexist definitions and treatment of women... and these distortions influence the Christian experience. (Johnson 1993: 10)

To bring ecofeminist critiques to religion is like bringing feminism to patriarchy; that is, there are many kinds of feminisms, and a variety of avenues for exploration. The joining together of ecology, feminism and theology is an interdisciplinary venture. Some put more emphasis on the ecological dimension, their main dialogue partner being the earth sciences; biology, geology, cosmology, ecology. For others the dialogue partner is the social sciences, meaning critical theories, social analyses, ethics and theories of liberation. And for others the primary reference point is theology – bible, traditions, doctrines, texts.

From the outset it is important to recognize that the ecofeminist challenge to theology is immense, and only beginning to be examined. Ecofeminist theology is developing, and predominantly through the efforts of specific individuals who offer possibilities and reinterpretations. These efforts are deliberated by others, who then add on, reshape or are inspired to go in alternative directions. *People* develop ecofeminist theology. As a student said in class, 'I realized that theology is not a truth out there but is done by people trying to figure things out just like me!'

Ecofeminism is engaging with several aspects of Christian theology, and five will be examined here. The first aspect is about where to start: the whole and the parts. The second aspect is about biblical studies, and the third is on the method of ecofeminist liberation theologies. The fourth is a discussion of multicultural and multi-religious ecofeminist perspectives, and the final aspect is on ecofeminist spiritualities. This will be followed by a summary and commentary.

The Whole and the Parts

In the interests of clarity I am creating a division between those who look at the whole of theology, and those who look at the parts. These are interdependent, of course, but such a division allows the possibility of seeing what is going on, and what is at stake. So we will begin with those who address the whole as a starting point.

The Whole of Theology

If the starting point is the whole of theology, then the search is not about how many resources exist within Christianity, but how the whole enterprise of theology can be done in light of the ecological crisis. Questions are asked about what central Christian notions might mean within an ecological paradigm. Several ecofeminist theologians have tackled this dimension by looking at creation.

Creation would seem to be an obvious starting point. Yet the actual doctrine of creation is a philosophical treatise about creation *ex nihilo* – out of nothing. It is predominantly about the the fact that life exists, and how God brought life 'out of the void'. The doctrine of creation is only about the creation of humans by God. The earth, although referred to, is not relevant.

Creation *stories*, however, are significant to Christianity and the ecological issue. Creation stories are about how life, all life, came into being. They give order and meaning, and often prescribe inter-human relationships, human–other animals positionings and the patterns within the natural world. Genesis is a creation story, understood in its day to be mythic, religious and cogent with the science of the day.

Sallie McFague reminds us that 'the world is our meeting place with God… it is wondrous, awesomely, Divinely mysterious' (McFague 1993: vii). Yet this very world is being rampantly destroyed. Her work is directed to theology, but with the goal of stemming the ecological devastation. She uses science as a starting point, with an emphasis on the process out of which the earth emerged, namely cosmology, and on evolutionary earth processes from which emerged all life. McFague realizes the significance of cosmology to both theology and to attitudes toward the natural world. With this in mind, she develops a theology of nature. She then moves among various assumptions of creation, anthropology, Christology, and eschatology, extending to each a metaphoric theology of the world as God's body. McFague understands the need to start with the whole, and then move to the parts.

Because creation stories are a mixture of mythology, religious claims, more or less science, and ultimate values, they are extremely influential in guiding civilizations, societies and individuals. Ruether surveyed three classical creation narratives: Babylonian, Hebrew, Greek and their relationship to Christian creation stories. From an ecofeminist analysis, she found core distortions, biases and limitations. She revealed their anti-women and anti-nature stances, and showed how these have influenced theological formulations of the doctrine of creation, eschatology and soteriology (Ruether 1992). She also found that Christianity could be reconnected to its earthly and cosmic dimensions through our contemporary scientific understanding of the earth and the cosmos. If so, it could provide a worldview from which we can discover and develop ethics oriented toward responding to the ecological crisis. Using the concepts and praxis of covenant, sacrament, and spirituality and politics, Ruether presents a renewed vision of the religious tradition within contemporary culture. We should thus embrace both the earth and God, or as she wrote, both Gaia and God.

Anne Primavesi also examines issues around creation stories and ecofeminism. Her findings are similar. She adds that there are obstacles in an overemphasis on Christology, within a multi-layered hierarchical paradigm (Primavesi 1991). She proposes replacing the traditional Christocentric hierarchical paradigm with an ecological paradigm. A scientifically-based evolutionary narrative is the preferred starting point. Through a reinterpretation of Genesis, Primavesi unearths a new creation story and through the motif of the 'spirit' of Genesis considers notions of sin, evil, redemption and salvation, doctrines of the Trinity, and the role of the Spirit in earth/human history.

These examples indicate that when theology is engaged with the ecological crisis in depth, there are major shifts in the very foundations. For ecofeminist theology to be adequate it must dialogue in depth with the earth sciences. This is an enormously significant shift in theology, and will be discussed thoroughly in Chapter Four.

What this work reveals is that to touch the foundations, or the whole, is to touch the parts, because the interpretation of the parts (anthropology, eschatology, Christology) flow from the whole. The foundational presuppositions are embedded within Christian interpretations of the world. For example many ecofeminists locate the theoretical origins of the crisis in the distortions and hierarchical dualisms of Euro-western culture and Christianity. These distortions have permeated the basic theoretical structures and orientations of much of theology. This begs the question of the whole. However a systematic ecofeminist reconstruction of the Euro-western Christian tradition is an immense task. Thus some begin by dialoguing with parts, or aspects of the tradition, examining and reinterpreting doctrines of God, the Trinity, and Christ. They also consider creation, revelation, anthropology, eschatology, notions of sin, salvation, redemption, the role of scripture, and authority. Although these are interconnected, some only look at a part, and even miss the whole! Still, the effect of such re-evaluation is somewhat like a domino effect, and eventually raises the thorny questions of the way theology is done, and what theology *is* anyway!

The Whole and the Parts: The Parts of Theology
a. *Doctrinal Reinterpretations: God*. How do we image God in an ecofeminist age? The monarchical, patriarchal male image of God has blinded us to the sacredness of the earth. It excludes women, all non-human animals and the earth from the sphere of the Sacred. The image of God as removed from, and other than, the earth is very different from a Creator Spirit Lifegiver intimately related to the earth (Johnson 1993: 10). Elizabeth Johnson suggests that God can be imaged as spirit, as within and among us, sustaining and creating all life in an ever-present dynamic of new possibilities. From here one can take this image and reinterpret anthropology, creation, scripture, spirituality, and ethics. This may seem to be theologically straightforward, and indeed appealing. However

the implications are decisive; that the notion of the Divine is active, present and moving through life and history means that we are not bound by the past. There is creative freedom in understanding and responding to the present; thus faithfulness to the past tradition is less important than faithfulness to the demands of the present. In addition, an understanding of the spirit as permeating all life challenges anthropocentrism and androcentrism.

b. *Anthropology, Creation, Sin, Grace and More*. The implications of ecofeminism for Christian anthropology are also being explored. What is the human person in an ecological age? An earth-centred and holistic approach emphasizes the interdependence of life. Humans are understood to be embedded in and a part of the natural world. Such interdependence can become an ethic or source from which to derive categories of human anthropology: relationship, mutuality, co-operation, radical dependence and interdependence, participation, responsibility, and the common good. A holistic and ecological paradigm counters the embedded tenets of anthropocentrism and hierarchical dualisms. However anthropology is anchored in the interrelated doctrines of creation, the human person and grace, and cannot be reinterpreted alone (Hinsdale 1990).

Sölle and Cloyes (1984) connect a creation theology based on the sacredness of the earth with the biblical tradition of historical liberation. Their work represents a blend of biblical, systematic and liberation theologies. They claim historical events of liberation precede creation, therefore soteriology – what salvation means – are the starting point for the reflection. For Sölle all theology must be in genuine solidarity with those oppressed through economical or political systems, alienated from meaningful work, internally divided between spirituality and sexuality, and estranged from the earth. Sölle challenges eco-theologians to realize that without a liberation tradition, ecological work is susceptible to 'cheap reconciliation' whereby we are asked to live as if we do not require freedom from unjust orders. Sölle asserts 'in the beginning was liberation', and there is no redemption without liberation. This raises the question of redemption.

In brief, Christianity has had two orientations towards life: one that it is inherently good, although incomplete, and the other that it needs partial or complete redemption. The goodness of creation has been shrouded by the redemption tradition. The latter emphasizes different notions of 'the fall', and overshadows the goodness of life with the claims that sin has permeated existence to differing degrees. Thus redemption is needed for salvation. The Christian tradition has interpreted itself predominantly in terms of sin and redemption. The division between creation and redemption, and the overemphasis on the latter, has cost the Christian tradition dearly. That creation is inherently good has been all but forgotten in the face of the innumerable interpretations of redemption and salvation. In addition, redemption usually refers only to humans; the rest is insignificant. These views rest on a foundation that humans are 'other' than the natural world, and do not belong in this order of reality. Humans will be redeemed from earth, resurrected into heaven – which is elsewhere. Although these are heady notions and involve extensive work to understand them, they are also common beliefs in Christian communities today. I noticed a beautiful bumper sticker recently that had the stunning image of the earth from space. As I got closer I read the words; 'Jesus, don't leave earth without him!' While a popular belief, it reveals that an anti-earth bias is blended into too many Christian core notions.

In response to the ecological crisis, there is a reclaiming of the wisdom that life is intrinsically and immeasurably good. The time has come to emphasize the goodness of all of creation. In ecotheology a creation-centred tradition is favoured over a fall/redemption, wherein all of life is understood as coming into fullness rather than in need of redemption. The meaning of the fall in an ecological age is also under scrutiny. Fall from what or where, we might ask? Fall into what? From paradise to sin? The matter of creation raises fundamental questions about redemption and salvation, and by extension the notions of sin and grace.

Ecofeminism situates sin within the interlocking oppressions of ethnicity, colonialism, class, gender, and the domination of the earth. Sin exists where life cannot thrive. Grace is found in liberating life and those held captive by the bonds of oppression. Is ecological ruin a sin? Is this a moment of grace where we can begin to know the sacred dimensions of the earth before it is too late? What if the life on earth severely diminishes? This leads toward eschatology, the questions of the final events of the world and its ultimate destiny. And then, what does heaven mean?

Eschatology is also studied through an ecofeminist lens.[10] Catherine Keller reflects on the connections between the 'wasting of the world' and historical notions of eschatology. She associates the doctrines of eschatology with creation. Eschatology is reoriented to mean that our eschatological task is to renew 'this Earth, this sky, this water', and to make a home for ourselves here. Keller reminds us that: 'We do not need a new heaven and Earth' (Keller 1990: 263).

---

10.   Catherine Keller, 'Women Against Wasting the World: Notes on Eschatology and Ecology' (1990); 'Talking About the Weather: The Greening of Eschatology' (1993). See also Primavesi, *From Apocalypse to Genesis* (1991: 67–84); Martha Dyson, 'Ecological Metaphors in Feminist Eschatology' (1990).

To take this further raises questions about the entrenched views of life after death and human resurrection.

What would the meaning of human resurrection be if humanity were accepted as an integral member of an earth community of life? Is all of the earth resurrected? Perhaps it is time to let go of the belief in human resurrection and life after death? Perhaps resurrection means a continual dying and rising to new life in the here and now? If the answer is yes, then we begin another level of pondering that brings us back to questions about the meaning of creation, anthropology, sin and eschatology. It raises other questions about the nature of religious language, symbols and metaphors. Is resurrection a 'fact' or is it the Christian insight that life does not end with death, that in some form nothing is lost? Perhaps it could be the Christian way of knowing that in the earth processes, nothing is wasted and everything is recycled and reborn in another form.

If we can stay with these questions, then even more emerge. What, for example, is the role of Christianity today, in a postmodern world of religious, cultural and worldview pluralities? How can we understand all these religious truths? If it is not possible for each religion to be equally true, and it is also not possible that one is truthful and the others are wrong, then we need to address all of this in a larger horizon of meaning. We need to have a greater understanding of the nature of religion, religious truths, and the insights, strengths and limits of each religion. Popular Christianity is often equated with a set of beliefs, rather than a faith orientation to life itself. Perhaps the essence of Christianity is a call to work for renewal and repair of the world. It could be oriented to the salvation of this world, drawing on socio-political and ecological analysis to inform a theology focused on praxis. Realistic hope lies in a consciousness that 'apocalypse is unacceptable, that causes are analysable, and that people can make a difference' (Keller 1993: 47). Here a blend between liberation, eschatology and hope are interwoven for the sake of all life on earth.

To address in any depth these theological parts – creation, anthropology, redemption, sin, grace – returns us again and again to the question of the whole of theology. Theological worldviews are just that – worldviews with interrelated parts in a whole stance about life itself. It is deep and rich, profoundly influential yet not straightforward.

Biblical Studies
When ecotheology and ecofeminists address scripture, a lot begins to happen. Much of scripture-based ecotheology has seized upon Genesis, and in particular the countless deliberations on dominion of the earth. The translations vary from the human being a good steward, manager or gardener, or as a

co-creator with God. Ecofeminists remain dubious of both this scriptural methodology and the reinterpretations. It keeps the hierarchical dualisms in place and misses the fundamental reality of human dependence on the earth. The theology behind stewardship is incompatible with a radical ecofeminist perspective because it claims a Divine-human relationship which preserves a human–earth division, thus hierarchy is maintained. Theologically, steward-ship signifies a shift within the present system rather than a vision of a new and different order (Ruether 1985: 206).

Ecofeminists tend to deal with a prior question than stewardship or even any scriptural interpretation, and that is why and how we look to the bible at all. There are numerous problems with the question of scripture from an eco-feminist viewpoint. One is about *how* the bible is used. As says Mieke Bal, 'The Bible, of all books, is the most dangerous one, the one that has been endowed with the power to kill' (Bal 1991: 14). The bible is patriarchal and often con-tinues to be interpreted through patriarchal, anthropocentric and androcentric beliefs. Feminist biblical scholarship has repeatedly found that 'the merest fragment of feminist biblical scholarship constitutes a challenge of established assumptions' (Bal 1989: 15; Milne 1995: 47–52). A second problem is about the role of the reader or interpreter. The issue of interpretation has become very important. The question is no longer what the bible means, or even why it means, but *how* it means (Milne 1995: 66). How do people make their interpretations of the bible? Can a text not lend itself in a direction that is not within the reader? A common feminist view is that it is the reader who makes – not takes – the meaning from the text. A third problem is about the truth and authority of scriptural texts; this is even more thorny. Feminist scholarship has revealed that the formation of the religious canon is foremost a question of power; texts became authoritative first, and then were deemed sacred and canonical (Pui-lan 1995: 17). Finally, for some feminists the bible cannot be reread, refurbished, rehabilitated or reinterpreted into an adequate spiritual source for women. (Milne 1993: 148). Feminist postmodern approaches can transform the way we relate to, interpret and understand the bible, but they cannot rescue the bible itself from patriarchy (Milne 1993: 164). In fact, some argue that the hierarchical dualisms that are a source of the current socio-ecological problems and critiqued by ecofeminists are inherent in the biblical sources of Christian theologies. The implications of ecofeminist biblical read-ings have yet to be explored in depth, and there are few samples to study (Eaton 2000: 54–72).

So what are ecofeminists to do with the bible? The usual route is to move from the quagmire of methods of biblical study to reinterpret biblical themes.

For example, the popular theme of 'spirit' can be expanded to include the earth. Primavesi combines a spirit theology with a fresh look at Genesis, and suggests that the 'Spirit of Genesis', a life-giving spirit of ecological creation and abundance, has been overlooked (Primavesi 1991). Others take the biblical theme of covenant, and reinforce the meaning that the covenantal community includes all species. If the covenant is between God and all of life, then right relations between humans and the earth will be maintained. This then acts as a framework for justice (Robb and Casebolt 1991: 18–21). The natural world becomes included in the history of creation, redemption and salvation.

Increasingly ecofeminists combine biblical motifs with earth sciences, for example with biology, geology and cosmology. For example, Anne Clifford uses biblical wisdom literature as a basis for an ecological theology of creation in a covenantal partnership of humans with non-humans (Clifford 1992: 65–92). Others emphasize wisdom as Sophia who provides a corrective to the hierarchical and dualistic relationship between the divine and creation. To really listen to Sophia 'immanent within nature as God's creation, means we will discover ourselves within rather than apart from our complex global ecosystem' (Clifford 1992: 90). In a similar vein, Primavesi suggests that Wisdom writings are a 'science of doxology', a direct appeal to the human mind to penetrate the order of the cosmos, and to know and love it. Wisdom invites contemplation of the earth, the bringing together of scientific knowledge and a profound sense of wonder and respect (Primavesi 1993: 2).

There has been an effort to recover the biblical theme of Jubilee. It offers ecological resources of letting the land lie fallow every seven years, and an economic paradigm of every forty-nine years equally redistributing the wealth. The creation narrative of Job and the insights in Ecclesiastes are rich with ecological possibilities. The prophetic and wisdom traditions offer a wealth of resources. There are specific teachings on a preferential option for the poor, ethics of the common good, and images of life abundant. There are also plenty of biblical resources in the justice and liberation traditions. All of these are open to reinterpretation, once the initial question of why we look to the bible is resolved.

Liberation Theology and Ethics
Ecofeminists are drawn to liberation theologies because of their emphasis on both the empirical and the cultural-symbolic aspects of reality and theology. Liberation theologies are also a combination of theoretical analysis and political activism. They begin with critical analyses of the particular social, political and economic relations. The hallmark of liberation theologies is a dedication to

reality, and reality is concrete and historical-bound (Harrison and Robb 1985: 245). For a liberationist, an analysis is theological if, and only if, it unveils or envisions our lives as a concrete part of the interconnected web of the social, the natural world, and the sacred. Liberation theology is capable of forging links between social justice and ecojustice.

The methodology of the liberationist traditions is useful, although as Brazilian ecofeminist theologian Ivone Gebara indicates, Latin American liberation theology is neither feminist nor ecological. Nor has it changed the patriarchal anthropology and cosmology upon which Christianity is based (Ress 1993: 12–13). To rectify this for ecofeminist liberation theologians, empirical resources are available from global ecofeminist efforts concerned with systemic patterns of domination, the global economic system, militarism, reproductive rights, biotechnology, and the development agenda. Ecofeminist theories, the analysis of domination as presented in Chapter Two, and the socio-political and philosophical frameworks also support liberation movements. An ecofeminist liberation theology oriented, not only to the perversions and rectifications of the ideological origins of the socio-ecological crisis, but to agency, moves theology into the political realm. Ecofeminist liberation theologies take many forms in many places, and because of its centrality to ecofeminist theology specific examples will be discussed in greater depth in the next chapter.

In general, several trends are occurring that merit mentioning here, such as doing theology from specific contexts, listening to those at the margins, and collaborating with women from around the world. Women of the South bring their voices, concerns and analyses to bear, and articles in ecofeminist theology are appearing in many parts of the world. Often they reveal that Christianity is never the same in two places, and is usually an amalgamation of many sub-traditions and cultures. These women show how an ecofeminist spirituality blends with earth-based images, such as from Asia and Africa, focussing particular attention on the cosmological aspects of the 'cosmos as God's womb' (Kyung 1994: 175–78). Aruna Gnanadason, from an Indian perspective, notes that the work for justice must now include the earth. As she states, 'creation is not a secondary issue.' Gnanadason draws from the 'dynamic feminine principle shakti' to argue that acts against creation break the spiritual bond between women and the natural world (Gnanadason 1994: 183). Such ecofeminist visions challenge both the global economic policy and the development agenda, and infuse theology with fresh images and analyses.

The World Council of Churches (WCC) is active in promoting ecofeminist perspectives. The WCC not only pursues social analysis and mounts campaigns for social reform; it also represents a major part of the Christian Churches, both Protestant and Orthodox. They recognize the need to develop a greater ecofeminist analysis, particularly in reference to the immense suffering of women and their land due mostly to the industrialized nations and their push for economic globalization. The familiar themes of women, peace, justice and integrity of creation came together in July 2003 to focus on the theme of eco-feminism, specifically ecofeminist theology. Ten women were brought together from Kenya, South Africa, India, Thailand, Hong Kong, Korea, Brazil, Chile, the United States and myself from Canada to deliberate on ecofeminist theology. After much discussion, the emphasis was placed on promoting local alternatives to the systems of corporate dominance. A desire was raised to analyse how specific communities and grassroots groups are thriving apart from the globalization agenda. Another desire was to support communities to form craft, marketing, and farmers co-ops that promote sustainable trade and agriculture. The role of cosmology and its relationship to everyday living was mentioned, and to begin to understand how women and indigenous people become agents of alternative economics that can also tap into the alternative ethics and cosmologies than those presently ruling the world.[11]

What was also striking at this event was that the often-used categories of power and privilege – North or South, elite or marginalized, people of colour and white folk, the west and the rest – were blurred. For example, within this small group there was a white American woman living in Chile, a Korean woman living in New York, a woman from Hong Kong living in eastern United States and an Indian woman living in Geneva. The cross-cultural boundaries were fluid. Issues of representation were also unclear. For example, who could speak for what groups of women? Who were the elite and who were the marginalized? In addition, while many, including myself, deride the anaemic, culturally insensitive and overly rational conceptual emphasis of the Euro-western intellectual traditions, everyone in the group, from Thailand to Brazil, did graduate theological studies in North America. Perhaps it is time to re-examine the customary lines of power and privilege with greater nuance. None-theless, these liberation voices are increasingly plural in numerous ways, and it is difficult to speak of ecofeminist theology as it is really a plethora of insights merging from ecology, feminism and multi-religious and cultural contexts.

Multicultural and Multi-Religious Perspectives
A few words need to be said about the desire to include more voices than those from Euro-western Christianity in ecofeminist religious efforts. Carol

---

11. Rosemary Radford Ruether attended the event, which was described in the *National Catholic Reporter*, Vol. 39, No. 36 (15 August 2003).

Adams' book *Ecofeminism and the Sacred* (1993) was a laudable effort that brought together ecofeminist religious voices from Buddhist, Hindu, Jewish, Christian, African-American, Neo-pagan, Native American and shamanic perspectives. The disciplinary mixture includes philosophical insights connecting ecofeminism, spirituality and political action. Elizabeth Green and Mary Grey edited a collection from European scholars entitled *Ecofeminism and Theology* written in Dutch, French and English (1994). It includes a range of non-mainstream viewpoints, such as Nordic versions of ecofeminism (Dagny Kaul), cosmic awareness in feminine sacred art (Caroline Mackenzie) and the daunting shape-shifting transmutation of theology to incorporate ecofeminism (Elizabeth Green). Another multi-religious ecofeminist work is *Women Healing Earth: Third World Women on Ecology, Feminism and Religion* (Ruether 1996). Essays from women in Latin America, Asia and Africa expand and complexify the standpoint of religious ecofeminist perspectives. These women present unique perspectives and context-specific critiques of androcentrism and resistance to the mutually reinforcing domination of women and the natural world. Here issues of ethnicity, class, global disparities and increasing impoverishment of peoples and land are prioritized over theoretical concerns of essentialism and 'exultant experiences of the rising moon and the seasonal wonders' (Ruether 1996: 3–7). A second contribution they bring is to recover spiritualities and practices from the indigenous roots in a pre-Christian past.

It is important to hear how distinct cultures, religions and people use ecofeminism in their own situations. From another vantage point, the book *Ecofeminism and Globalization: Exploring Culture, Context and Religion* (Eaton and Lorentzen 2003) points out that ecofeminism is done differently in distinct places. In some instances ecofeminism does not shed light on or assist the women-nature nexus. It is not always helpful in alleviating problems for women and ecological stress. This is an equally important contribution to the interface between ecofeminism, cultures and religions.

The multi-religious voices are needed and welcomed to the conversation. They provide a reality check in several ways. The first is a grounding in an awareness of the daily relationship between many women and the natural world; issues of toxins in air, water and soil, garbage dumps where people live, economic exploitation from globalization and stories of resistance and celebration. They provide concrete connections between theory and praxis, North and South, affluent and poor, and the actual life and death struggles of the many women of the world. They also show that concepts such as ecofeminism are not transportable everywhere. The second reality check is a reminder to all that 'religion' is religions; multiple, distinct and dissimilar. The world is full of religions, and the exchanges are innumerable. Theologizing about religion has not caught up to these lived realities. Each religion must now be understood in its own contexts and in relation to the many other religions of the world, past and present. They can no longer be self-referencing and isolated. And third, the ecological crisis is generating profound levels of analysis, and effecting a thorough re-thinking of religions and their cultural roles. Many of the attitudes towards the natural world have been shaped by religious worldviews. This challenges each tradition to revisit its presuppositions, discover its particular strengths and lacunae, and find resources that encourage benevolent human–earth relations.

Ecofeminist Spiritualities
Ecofeminist spiritualities are yet another bounteous aspect of ecofeminism and theology/religion. It is often through spirituality that religion enters the interdisciplinary ecofeminist roundabout. Ecofeminist spiritualities transcend theological and religious boundaries, and proliferate in images such as Gaia, Mother Earth, Sophia, Christ(a), Spirit, Goddess, Divine Matrix, and Cosmic Egg. The abundance of ecofeminist spiritualities defies description. They are found within traditional religions, Goddess, Wiccan and indigenous traditions, within reinterpreted versions, or are entirely new. At times these ecospiritualities are contemporary versions of old spiritualities that were discredited, such as parts of Celtic or shamanic traditions. They are expressed in rituals and ceremonies, vision quests, retreats, dance, prayers and worship, academic courses, publications, workshops and conferences. A good percentage of ecofeminist spiritualities, as practised, is an amalgamation; images and practices from one tradition are mixed with another, and interpreted in altogether new ways unrelated to their origins.

For most the ecological dimension of spirituality rests on the presupposition that the earth is sacred, and that the immanent presence of the sacred within nature evokes respect for all living things. Interconnectedness, webs of relations, interdependence, mutually enhancing patterns of existence, and the subjectivity of life itself are all terms commonly used to reach beyond the mechanistic, technical, and anthropocentric worldviews. There is a resurgence of nondualistic spiritualities, with an emphasis on the wisdom traditions from all religions for ecological insights. There is an interest in cosmology – meaning a sense of the whole, the unfolding story of the universe, ultimate source of revelation – as the fundamental framework in which to situate the wisdom traditions. In some cases there is a reclaiming of a 'feminine' principle, and elsewhere a deconstruction of it. It is important to acknowledge that the current period, while marked with crises, is also one of spiritual searching and renewal. These efforts gather insights from Buddhist, indigenous, Native American, Goddess, Christian, Jewish, Moslem, Hindu and Wiccan teachings.

Women are engaged in creative exploration of fresh images that are emerg-ing from the cultural contexts of the ecological crisis and the feminist move-ment. For many, actions to preserve and protect the earth are considered to be part of one's spiritual practice. Ecofeminist liturgies are appearing at the inter-section, and fresh resources are becoming available (Neu 2002).

It is a trustworthy sign that these spiritualities do not fit into any theological box. Equally, it is premature to judge these invigorating movements, as through them spirituality is enlivened in Euro-western culture. Post- and current Chris-tian women and men are finding themselves within myriad ecofeminist expres-sions. But while there has been a proliferation of ecofeminist spiritualities, there has been little religious or systemic analysis of the phenomenon. This may not be feasible or desirable, as ecofeminism represents a 'new' insight, and may need to be explored rather than theologically scrutinized.

However, for the ecofeminist roundabout as a whole, the presence of spiri-tualities can be a problem. Due to their fluid nature, the many symbols and images, an unclear theoretical base, the crossovers between religions and cul-tures, and the limited political analyses, spirituality is considered at times to be too vague and not helpful. Some theoretical ecofeminist critiques dismiss the spiritual aspect for being apolitical, essentialist and irrelevant to cultural trans-formation. This has led to a confused and confusing barrage of critiques against ecofeminism and the spiritual dimensions.[12] It has also meant that any reli-gious or theological contribution is met with caution, which is unfortunate because religion has much to offer to the larger intersection of ecofeminism. Nonetheless, 'scorned, trivialized or ignored by many in the academy, the strength of ecofeminism is in the streets… inspired by earth-based spirituality' (Seager 1993: 251).

---

12.   For an interesting description of this problem in ecofeminism see Mary Mellor, *Breaking the Boundaries* (1992); and Joni Seager, *Earth Follies: Coming to Feminist Terms with the Global Environmental Crisis* (1993). Seager, quoting from Biehl, assumes that the core ecofeminist question is 'are women closer to nature than men?' and from there deconstructs the question, and the presumed answer that women are indeed more 'natural'. Ecofeminism is then discredited for being apolitical, universalizing, indistinguishable from the conservative patriarchal ideology of women and nature, and is, in general, 'skating on ideologically thin ice'. However, Seager, like Biehl and Westra, have not studied the bulk of ecofeminism, and dismiss the whole based on a few contributions. Although the same strands of essentialism, motherhood peace politics, and apolitical perspectives are easily found within the feminist discourse, feminism is not dismissed. To the contrary, ecofeminism is charged with being non-feminist! For criticisms of Biehl's work, which is frequently and unfortunately cited as being an accurate representation of ecofeminism, see Val Plumwood, 'The Atavism of Flighty Females: Review of *Finding Our Way*' (1992: 36).

Summary

So much more could be presented. The intersection of ecofeminism, theology and religion is itself a roundabout. As this chapter progressed further into the intersection, it is evident that our customary religious and theological categories need to be flexible to move with these new insights and collaborations. For example, one women's religious community I know redesigned their entire chapel from an ecofeminist perspective. They carved a primordial egg out of which came the diversity of creature-kind that inhabits the land, air and waters across Canada, such as ancient coiled-shell crustaceans and blue-green algae. This carving is womb-like, a place to be in touch with the Divine mother, the creator God, and 'the Word made flesh'. The altar's base is the remains of an ancient nearby tree stump. The elements of earth, air, fire and water are carved from the cross at the four cardinal directions with the representation of the seasons. The whole chapel embraces and echoes the richness of these ancient symbols in every detail, as well as the ecosystem where it is located in Niagara Falls, Ontario. The Christian symbolism is honoured within the larger context of the earth and the universe. Overall the chapel is an amazing blend of symbols, traditions, expressions and original insights. These new expressions reflect a new consciousness, one that the traditional theological categories cannot contain.

Ecofeminist theologies are plural, and they address the parts and the whole. In one sense they are an intersection within the larger roundabout of ecofeminism. Each contribution to ecofeminism influences further efforts. What was presented here was only a snapshot of the traffic at the intersection!

Critique and Commentary

These five areas of ecofeminist theology (the parts and the whole, biblical studies, ecofeminist liberation theologies, multi-religious and multicultural perspectives, and spiritualities) have been presented to acknowledge the diverse approaches to unite ecology, feminism and theology. Many areas overlap. To step back and see what is occurring, there are three particular considerations that emerge; the challenge, the content and the method.

a. *Theological Challenge*. First it is important to recognize that the ecofeminist encounter with theology is profound and permeates all layers of theological reflection and praxis. The extent of the ecofeminist challenge to and confrontation with classical theology is only in the initial states of articulation. Ecological and feminist problems cannot simply be added to theology, for two reasons. The first is that theology, in general, contains both anti-women and anti-nature elements. A second, as discovered by feminists, is that one cannot just remove the offending parts and think all will be fine! The very way of doing theology – of asking questions, of the kinds of questions, and the way to go about seeking answers – is found wanting in the face of both the feminist and ecological challenges.

b. *Theological Content.* Of the theological considerations that are raised when ecofeminism comes into contact with theology, a basic one is about theological content. Content refers to the combination of religious language and meaning. As mentioned, one simply cannot add ecology and feminism to theology. Many questions emerge as to the meaning of theological terms. If the human has language to express a sense of the divine, how do we reconceptualize the distinction between humans and the other than human natural world? Classical Christianity maintains not only a distinction but an ontological rift between humans and the world, between the earth and God. Yet in much of ecofeminist and ecotheology, the Divine and the human are often seen as embedded within the natural world and within natural processes. The earth community is revelatory, a 'divine milieu'. This then raises questions about God, and where and how we encounter, or know anything about God. What is the role and status of creation from an ecofeminist viewpoint? The tradition advocates panentheism, meaning that the Divine is understood to be within and around us, (pan-theism) and also beyond (pan-en-theism). Panentheism reminds us that the Mystery of the Divine is beyond our understanding, and beyond the phenomenal world. Perhaps the way of asking and answering the question about God and the natural world is different from an ecofeminist perspective. Or perhaps the categories of pantheism and panentheism only work for conceptual distinctions, as a way of thinking, but are just that – a certain way of thinking. These categories may not reflect 'reality'. Perhaps our categories of thinking about the natural world, the role of humanity and the Divine are neither related to our actual experiences of these, nor to an ecosystems understanding of the world. Ecofeminism reveals that such theological concepts are too abstract and not grounded in the many-layeredness of human experience. Nonetheless, if the natural world is revelatory and there is a need for a religious sensitivity towards the earth, and if previous theological language and categories cannot accommodate these experiences and notions, then the theological categories must be changed or invented. This is one reason why ecofeminists increasingly look to earth sciences and evolutionary cosmology.

A related consideration is that of the transcendence and immanence of the Divine. Usually immanence is stressed within an ecological and feminist theology, although not exclusively, because the immanence of the Divine is imprinted within the evolution of the earth. Here spirit and matter are intimately, and indistinguishably, bound together in a life-process.

Other questions emerge, for example, about the over-emphasis on redemption and the neglect of creation. How is redemption to be understood in an ecological or cosmological paradigm? From one viewpoint the earth needs to be redeemed from the human race! How are redemption and resurrection related? Is resurrection a metaphoric motif, a paradigmatic understanding, a theme of liberation, or is the resurrection of the body (human and non-human) a substantive eschatological reality? Or is resurrection a phenomenon in the Spirit, pervasive throughout all the universe, meaning life always emerges from death? Is resurrection always Christocentric? What about the many world religions, and their equally compelling truths? Many believe that all theological language is metaphoric and symbolic, and represents only tentative images and expressions. Theological language should be deeply rooted in religious experiences, where expression is a secondary process. Thus theological content, that is language and meaning – resurrection, redemption, the Spirit, Christology – is only relevant in the to and fro from deep religious experiences, which are always beyond language.

The alienation between humans and the natural world in Christian cultures is not easily rectified. This alienation is implanted within the worldview, value systems and cultural beliefs and practices. Many Christians find sensing the Sacred in the natural world is less real than their beliefs and traditions. As a result some Christians are difficult to mobilize in the face of the ecological crisis.

c. *Theological Method*. Ecofeminist theologians insist on the need to abolish the hierarchical dualisms because these have thwarted the possibilities of mutually enhancing relationships among humans and with the earth community. From an ecofeminist perspective spirit and matter, body and mind, reason and emotion, for example, are seen as interconnected rather than dualistic. The superiority of reason over emotion, culture over nature, or objective over subjective are rejected outright. Even the actual divisions themselves are often discounted. Much of theology has been done through the lens of a hierarchical and dualistic worldview. If one rejects the worldview out of which the theology is done, then it puts into question not only the theological content but the whole way of doing theology! It becomes a question of method.

It seems that those who take the magnitude of the ecological crisis seriously tend to scrutinize Christianity itself in more radical ways than those who are either defending Christianity or simply retrieving resources. Drastic changes are called for. The reshaping of religion(s) remains the substantive and more arduous task. Limitations exist in reworking some traditions, such as Christianity, which have accumulated misogynist notions and anti-ecological interpretation. The discontinuity required from such core stances, from both ecological and feminist evaluations, is daunting. There is a tension between how far a tradition can be stretched and reinterpreted, and the need for new religious sensitivities that can respond to the socio-ecological plight. To some extent, this tension mirrors the feminist ambivalence with patriarchal religions, among those who modify existing systems, those who continue the analytic (deconstruction) work and those who create new traditions.

Ecofeminist efforts at reinterpretation without addressing either the fundamental presuppositions or the theological methodology are a dangerous pursuit, given the magnitude of the crisis. Religions have immense power to create and sustain cultural patterns. Few ecofeminist theologians deal with the radical discontinuity that both the ecological and feminist evaluations together pose to theology.

This is hardly a facile task. Even when the need for systematic deconstruction of the foundations of the tradition is called for, reconstruction typically is offered with respect to particulars. Again the dialectic between the whole and the parts surfaces, and either way Christianity does not move with ease into an ecofeminist perspective.

Conclusion

Ecofeminism and theology are an active aspect of the ecofeminist intersection. Christian values and worldviews have been the prevailing influences in shaping Euro-western cultures. Characteristics of these cultures, among other things, are the subjugation of women and ecological ruin. Thus it is crucial to examine the relationships between Christianity, ecology and feminism. Ecofeminist theologies are well placed to expose the layers of the history, renounce the anti-earth and misogynist elements, and retrieve and create new traditions. As more ecofeminist theologians enter the traffic roundabout, there are three traffic tips that would help them navigate the routes.

Ecofeminism is comprised of many divergent positions, different approaches and several levels of critical analysis. The first tip is that ecofeminist theologians need to be explicit about their understanding of the women–nature nexus and the relationships between women and the natural world. They need to be aware of the extent to which the concerns within ecofeminist discourse (epistemology, essentialism, ethnicity and class issues, theory and action, etc.) are pursued. As there is no one ecofeminist perspective, any ecofeminist theology would be served best by knowing the full spectrum of ecofeminisms.

Second, often ecofeminist theology takes its cues from ecofeminist theory in which the cultural-symbolic issues are prevalent and steers away from the global ecofeminist discourses on the material connections. This translates into the fact that few have addressed issues such as militarism, bio-, agro- or repro-ductive technologies, multinational corporations and globalization, debt and trade, free trade zones, life-form patents, etc. They have not moved into the realm of global political feminist or ecofeminist praxis. While we need to attend to the perversions and rectifications of various religious interpretations and methods, the accelerating ecological crisis and the strenuous material relation-ships between women and the natural world augment.

Third, to acknowledge the socio-ecological crises, to 'green' Christianity, and discuss endlessly the paradigm shift needed, does not confront either the crises or challenge the power structures. As Beverly Harrison states, misogyny's real force arises only when women's concrete power is manifested (Harrison 1985: 5). Ecofeminist liberation theologies that bring together ecological, feminist and global political/social analyses force theology out of the ivory tower and the protected parish into the harsh streets of concrete reality and its transformation. Only the liberationist streams, from around the world, yet to be fully developed, have the ability to move theology into this realm. The players of imperialist globalization or the World Bank do not care whether Wisdom/Sophia was present in Genesis, or that the Christian eschatological doctrines are distorted. But they will care if Christians, inspired and empow-ered by a new understanding of Wisdom and eschatology, resist the efforts of the World Bank, the World Trade Organization and the International Monetary Fund to prevent ecological ruin. It has suited both theology and the culture that religion remain an internal, personal and private affair. Thus, to evaluate eco-feminist theological work, one measure is whether the approach can move the effort into the work of resistance, vision and reconstruction. Two particular paths in the ecofeminist roundabout are of interest in this regard; the dialogue with the earth sciences and the emerging global work in ecofeminist liberation theologies. They are the topic of the next chapter.

Chapter Four

From the Cosmos to the City:
Evolution and Politics

The exploration of ecofeminism and theology has shown that to reinterpret theological categories from an ecofeminist viewpoint is challenging. As seen in the previous chapter, some people examine systematic theology and try to stretch basic tenets to incorporate ecofeminist viewpoints. Others offer fresh interpretations of biblical themes, or use liberation theories. However many theologians have realized that the very foundations of theology are inadequate to address the ecological crisis. They consider that the usual starting points for theology – scriptural texts, doctrines, symbols and ethics – are insufficient to deal with this level of crisis. They have turned to other conversation partners, and are reshaping both the whole and the parts of ecofeminist theology. The first partnership is between the earth sciences and theology. The second involves social-political analysis and social transformation, with attention to multicultural and multi-religious aspects. The bulk of ecofeminist theologians work in one or both of these streams. This chapter looks at each of these in turn.

The Role of Science in Ecofeminist Theologies

Religion without science is blind: Science without religion is lame.

(Albert Einstein)

As the ecological crisis worsens, and as theologians reflect more deeply, many see the need to rethink their responses in light of the earth sciences, especially that of cosmology and evolutionary biology. These are related to each other in that cosmology offers the larger context of the earth's emergence within the universe. Evolutionary biology provides the context of the emergence of life on earth. What theologians are discovering is that when the starting point changes from theology to evolutionary science, the theological contributions change dramatically. Many ecofeminist and ecotheologians work together with this combination of science and theology.

Those who engage seriously with religion and the ecological crisis soon realize that the Christian tradition has not been able to deal effectively with evolution; neither the history of cosmogenesis – the cosmos continually coming into being – nor the evolution of life on earth. If one takes either as a starting point, there are major consequences for religious understanding and Christian theology. Theologian John Haught considers that much of the reluctance of theology to address the ecological crisis in depth stems from a prior reluctance to think about evolution (Haught 1993: 32). The significance of evolution is only beginning to dawn on religious thinkers.

Evolution and Theology
Christian theology has divorced itself from the natural world. Ecotheologians try to repair this rupture. They retrieve parts of the tradition that are 'eco-friendly', reclaim lost elements such as a reverence for the natural world, rework existing symbols and teachings, and construct new viewpoints. With these collective efforts we can identify the transformative and prophetic insights and affirm the particular values that will assist Christians. However the reality of evolution raises new questions.

If we begin our theological reflection within an evolutionary framework, then we must begin with the history of the earth and of life on earth. The cosmos is approximately twelve to thirteen billion years old, and the earth is between four and five billion years of age. What is known of the emergence of life on earth is that it is immensely complex and sophisticated. Humans are latecomers onto the earth scene, having taken hundreds of thousands of years to develop. Our ancestors are primates, as are we.[1] In addition, given the era of the dinosaurs, where they were the reigning animal for over 160 million years, we must ask ourselves why we think that humans are the reference point for

---

1.   Evolution is accepted here as an accurate description of life on earth. Although all the aspects of the evolutionary process are not known precisely, there is no doubt here that evolution, meaning an incredibly complex process of the emergence of life through sequences of transformations, adaptability, creativity and ingenuity, best describe the existence of life. Given this creationism, meaning that God created humans apart from other animals, or any belief that humans are inherently separate from the earth, is rejected. Views that the earth is much younger than four billion years are rejected. For further discussion see Sandra Alters and Brian Alters, *Defending Evolution in the Classroom: A Guide to the Creation/Evolution Controversy* (2001); John Livingston, *Rogue Primate* (1994).

all of creation! An evolutionary starting point means that we need to rethink everything, including ourselves, within this large historical horizon.

Although timely, indeed popular, to reiterate that 'the earth is our home', the greater task is to allow our theological understanding to be transformed by this insight. The earth, ever emerging with increasing complexity, differentiation and interdependence, is the primary reality out of which humanity originated. Humanity is one species among many, coming into being within a process of complex experimentations with life on earth. To integrate evolution into religious and ecological perspectives is to accede to the fact that humans evolved from primates, and ultimately from the earth's inner processes. While this 'fact' is basically accepted, the implications have little impact. Most human communities live as if any history prior to human civilizations is irrelevant and inconsequential. In addition most industrialized societies refuse to accept the ultimate dependence on and priority of the earth's life systems. Yet, the earth is primary, the human derivative, as Thomas Berry often comments.

To consider earth history as a decisive framework is to perceive that religious consciousness is an emerging process within the larger evolutionary processes of the earth. From an evolutionary starting point the task is to situate the genesis and specific histories of each religion within the history of the earth. To situate our religious traditions – the myriad expressions of the sacred, their moral cores and codes, and magnificent rituals and symbols – within the evolutionary processes of the earth prevents us from situating earth history within the boundaries of our religious traditions. We are accustomed to our religious frameworks being the definitive references. Yet religious stories are a late development even within the human story and especially in the earth's story. In shifting the starting point to the evolutionary processes, we can begin to see the emergence of earth as a sacred story. The earth reveals the sacredness and genius of life, and the revelatory dimensions of the earth. We can discern that our religious 'truths' and 'revelations' must be understood differently. They are a kind of truth that is deeply symbolic and indispensable. Yet this is a new religious moment, a threshold of religious consciousness in which we have creative and novel opportunities for religious awareness. It is a unique opportunity in human/earth history.

However, evolution is an enormous threat to the worldview of modernity, and especially to conservative Christians who advocate 'creationism'. Creationism represents a range of views that does not accept much of the evolutionary evidence from science. Their argument is based on theological grounds. They have any number of publications, programs and websites, and make many claims. Three in particular are relevant here. One is that the earth is not nearly as old as scientific evidence claims. Two, that humans did not evolve from primates. The few who might concede that primates preceded humans think that there was a special intervention from God to separate humans from primates. And three, that all of the earth processes exist for the purpose of humans and their development. At the extreme end they separate entirely humans from the earth in both origin and destiny. As recently as May 2004, United States President George W. Bush stated on public radio that, 'Humans are not animals. We did not come from nor belong to this earth. We are created by God to have superiority over all life on earth.'

An acceptance of biological evolution as the basic understanding of the emergence of life is under siege in North America by creationists.[2] Evolution is touted as an unprovable theory. It is put on equal par with creationism, or rejected outright. Currently over fifty per cent of the United States public believes that God created humans as we are today (Alters and Alters 2001: 50). This is from the same culture where over half of the population believe that humans co-existed with dinosaurs (Alters and Alters 2001)! The Christian right is taking legal action to remove evolution from the science (not religion!) curriculum in schools and universities, and have been successful in eleven states thus far and are gaining ground in Canada. This reveals the level of confrontation between religion and evolution. The consequences will be devastating to an in-depth appreciation of the ingenuity of life and to fostering ecological sensitivity. It is further evidence of the irrationality of some religious worldviews, predominantly Christian, and to what lengths people will go to defend their worldviews and beliefs, however erroneous.

The impact of evolution on religion is both nuanced and complex. It is a serious matter for those resisting religious literalism and fundamentalism. This form of Christianity lacks a historical consciousness, operates from a narrow worldview, and refuses to use rational modes of inquiry. The debate around evolution is now a political force at the intersection of religion and ecology. Ecofeminist theology will gain no ground until it comes to terms with evolution and fundamentalist Christianities.

Cosmology and Evolution

> No science in the twentieth century has altered the human image of the self, earth, universe as drastically and permanently as astronomy. [...] No future

2.   Creationists are Christians who believe that God made humans in the recent past, evolution may apply to the earth but not to humans. Creationists vary in their beliefs as to the age of the earth, and how literally they interpret the bible. They are most prevalent in the United States.

psychology, anthropology, or theology will shape any convincing interpretations of human life without reference to the discoveries of modern cosmology.

(Denis Walsh)

If we extend the starting point of reflection from the history of the earth to the history of the universe out of which the earth evolved, we gain a further perspective and new resources. The term we use for this is cosmology, and many ecofeminist theologians work in the area of evolution and cosmology.

Cosmology has several meanings. It is about the evolving universe, the natural world and the human place within this horizon of reality. Cosmologies are also cultural stories about the universe, the earth and the role of the human. In the past and in some isolated societies today the scientific understanding of the universe is the same as the cultural story. Cosmology is that larger scheme of things, defined as a combination of natural science, philosophy, ethics and religion, in short, a worldview. It is the story – meaning, values, worldview – out of which people live their lives. Ecofeminist theologian Ruether describes cosmology as:

> [...] a view of the relation of humans to the rest of nature, their relation to each other in society, and their relation to the ultimate foundational source of life (the divine). They have been blueprints for what today we would call a combined scientific, social-ethical, and theological-spiritual worldview. (Ruether 1992: 32)

Cosmology reflects the cultural assumptions about the nature of the world (Tucker and Grim 1993). Cosmologies, as cultural myths or narratives, deeply influence the formation of social order, and affect how human–earth relations are to be conducted (McFague 1993). Thomas Berry is the primary mentor in this work in cosmology although it has been taken up by hundreds of religious, ecological and political thinkers and activists (Berry 1988, 2001). Matthew Fox has been influential in challenging theology to address both cosmology and the ecological crisis. He has developed creative theological tools and frameworks to inspire both vision and action. His work in creation spirituality has been of great benefit around the world. Theological responses to the ecological crisis are oriented increasingly towards questions of cosmology (Rasmussen 1993: 174).

Anne Clifford argues that theology needs to recover the universality of its tasks, with a further enlargement of theological horizons to attend to cosmology, by reinstating the cosmos into the realm of the sacred. Such a cosmic theology, according to Clifford, would be involved in the following:

> [...] deepening in the 'coherence of worldview' in which the continuity within creation – humans and all earth's life forms within the totality of cosmic processes – will be appreciated and reverenced in the light of God. [...and] a shared

> commitment to the ecological well-being of that part of the cosmos that we share
> and reverence as gift. (Clifford 1992: 33)

Many others argue eloquently for a cosmological perspective. They see the
need for a narrative that includes purpose and could assist in the reshaping of
our cultural vision.

Cosmology and the Ecological Crisis

With the rise of modernity as a worldview, Euro-western cultures dropped
cosmology as a horizon out of which we comprehend our lives. Given the
development of a dualistic and hierarchical worldview, and the rifts between
science and theology, cosmology is now usually only discussed in scientific and
mechanistic terms. The cosmos and the earth are presented to us in a machine-
like manner. They are not alive and have no intrinsic value. The prevailing
worldview is anthropocentric to an extreme. It barely includes the earth, and if
so only as a resource.

The effort to reacquaint ourselves with evolution, cosmology and their role
in orienting human actions has revealed that within the ecological crisis there
is also a crisis of worldview: of the meaning, values, origins and purpose of
life, and the role of humanity within the scheme of life. The story or worldview from which we live our lives is both outdated and dysfunctional. Berry
writes: 'The deepest crises experienced by any society are those moments of
change when the story becomes inadequate for meeting the survival demands
of a present situation. Such, it seems to me, is the situation we must deal with
in this late twentieth century' (Berry 1988: xi).

At the root of the ecological crisis is a profound sense of futility about the
cosmic venture, developed particularly through modern science. As a consequence, the universe and the natural world no longer held intrinsic value.
Nature was deprived of all qualities with which the human spirit could feel a
sense of kinship.

> The world as a whole was thus disenchanted… Hence no role exists in the
> universe for purposes, values, ideals, possibilities, and qualities, and there is no
> freedom, creativity, temporality or divinity. There are no norms, not even truth,
> and everything is ultimately meaningless. (Ray Griffin 1988: 3)

This view is propelling us towards an unprecedented ecological crisis for
which we are wholly unprepared. The mythic assumptions about the nature of
reality, which go largely unexamined, 'continue to nourish our toleration of ecological disintegration' (Haught 1993: 14). We do not have sufficient resources
within our prevailing understanding of the world to respond to this level of

Nyack College Library

crisis. Some would say that in the face of the ecological crisis, Euro-western cultures are ethically destitute (Sylvan and Bennett 1994).

The present era is the ending of the worldview of modernity, and although its momentum is ongoing, it will not carry us into a new and better world (Toulmin 1990: 3). In fact, the continuation of modernity 'threatens the very survival of life on our planet' (Ray Griffin 1988: xi). The larger cultural transformations that are occurring, including the new cosmology and its implications, can be described as essentially crises of perception. The major problems of our time – threats of war, ecological ruin, poverty, injustices and starvation – are different facets of a crisis of an outdated cosmology or worldview (Capra 1994: 334). We need a deep shift in cosmology that challenges the disenchanted view that the universe is pointless, lacks any ultimate purpose, has no transcendent origins, and has no divinely shaped destiny. What is occurring is a profound epistemological and cultural reformation; that is, recasting the worldview of modernity. This reflects the need 'to envisage postmodern ways of relating to each other, the rest of nature, and the cosmos as a whole' (Griffin 1988: xi). We need to restore cosmology, and attempt to return to thinking about the universe as a whole and integrated reality. Some conditions for a postmodern cosmology are that:

> ... our understandings of humanity and nature are integrated with practice in view, including reinserting humanity, and, in fact, life as a whole, back into nature, and regarding our fellow creatures not merely as means to our ends but as ends in themselves. (Ray Griffin 1988: 31)

These two aspects of cosmology – the alluring universe and the construction of worldviews – are both related to the emerging sensitivity towards the natural world, and the development of ecofeminist spiritualities. While current interest in cosmology extends into several realms, the focus here is on the emerging ecological worldviews grounded in an evolutionary cosmology; that is the new or postmodern ecological cosmology. [3] It is a developing viewpoint

---

3.   However, all work in cosmology is not relevant. Past and present study of cosmology has been embedded in the predominant patriarchal suppositions. The prevailing dualisms, the hierarchical thinking, the often exclusive language, and the astonishing lack of methodological analysis are disconcerting at best. The presuppositions of the worldviews remain obscure. The work often is oblivious to feminist analyses. The surfeit of cosmological anthologies with virtually all male authors continues to keep cosmology within restricted parameters. For example see; Clifford Matthews and Roy Abraham Varghese (eds.), *Cosmic Beginnings and Human Ends* (1995); Ted Peters (ed.), *Cosmos as Creation: Theology and Science in Consonance* (1989); John Mangum (ed.), *New Faith-Science Debate: Probing Cosmology, Technology and Theology* (1989). I agree with the concern of James Moore that the renewed

within ecotheology, and one which is at an interdisciplinary juncture of science, spirituality, philosophy, reconstructive postmodernism, and at times feminism. Cosmology is involved in recasting the worldview of modernity, including a profound epistemological and cultural reformation that may help change our thinking about the earth. Ecofeminists join these efforts to analyse and transform. They bring crucial insights in the move beyond a mechanistic worldview to a holistic postmodern ecological cosmology or worldview.

Christianity, Evolutionary Cosmology and the Ecological Crisis
Prior to Teilhard de Chardin, Thomas Aquinas, a twelfth-century theologian, was the last influential theologian to consider cosmology as central to theology. Cosmology has diminished in theological significance and been replaced with a human-centred focus. Theology became dissociated from cosmology and science. For centuries the predominant theological focus has been on anthropocentric and individualistic concerns primarily in relationship to doctrines of redemption although now entrenched in all theological discourses. Theology neglected a meaningful doctrine of creation and with it an awareness of the natural world. When cosmology disappears, so does a consciousness of the earth and of the whole context of life. This loss is associated directly with the ecological crisis.

To conceive of Christianity in light of an evolutionary cosmology calls for substantial re-evaluations of some foundational theological assertions (Haught 1999; Primavesi 2000). Although not alone, Christianity in particular has developed an extremely anthropocentric worldview, even to the point that the destruction of the natural world does not register as alarming either physically or spiritually. The operative Christian worldview emphasizes that human origin and destiny are elsewhere. The earth and the natural world are seen at best as resources, having no inherent or sacred presence. The Christian faith has belittled the earth as a primary religious reality. The earth history is excluded from salvation history, and at times the earth is seen as malevolent and antagonistic to salvation. The excessive concern for the redemptive process has concealed the realization that the disintegration of the natural world is also the destruction of the primordial manifestation of the divine (Fox 1983, 1991).

At the basis of the domination of the earth is a human refusal to accept the conditions of life: finitude, mortality and vulnerability, suggests Gebara

interest in cosmology from some quarters is a re-emergence of patriarchy. James Moore, *Cosmology and Theology: the Re-Emergence of Patriarchy* (Paper presented at annual meeting of the American Academy of Religion, Theology and Science Group, Washington, D.C., Nov. 1993).

(Ruether 2000). Great efforts are put into trying to escape the inescapable. Most notions of Christian resurrection, redemption and salvation are about bypassing these conditions. We try to dominate those aspects that expose the limits of life. The Christian tradition constantly tries to 'lift' humanity above the earth and the limits it represents, and ultimately beyond death. This, in turn, has caused distortions at the level of foundational theological precepts. Christianity has been built on a theological structure grounded on the impulse to dominate, exploit and conquer in order to escape life's conditions. The result is a 'fall into domination' in order to squelch those aspects, such as illness and disabilities, or to oppress those peoples who represent – to the dominating group – the weaker elements of humanity, such as women, Indigenous peoples, all other than white ethnic groups, etc. As a result there is a diminished Christian awareness of the tremendous gift of life and consciousness, of myriad and spectacular life forms and human diversity, of the genius of life itself, and of a sacred indwelling presence in the natural world. All of this is creation; an immeasurably precious gift, that includes finitude, mortality and vulnerability. The refusal to accept life on its terms is one of the central causes of the ecological crisis, and of the intricate systems of domination and exploitation.

Ecotheologians, one after the other, have been compelled to deal with the Christian emphasis on humanity's transcendence over, and thrust to desacralize, the natural world (Pearson 2002: 51). Primavesi writes 'the fears inspired by the loss of the theological anthropocentricity, or even the suspicion of its loss, explains why ecotheology seems to have lost its appeal for some theologians' (Primavesi 2000: note – The Way – 63). The biblical-redemptive story rather than the creation/evolutionary story has been chosen as the primary context of understanding and finding meaning in life. Because a sense of the divine is derived extensively from biblical sources, an awareness of the revelation of the divine in the natural world has been all but lost for many Euro-western Christians.

A profound re-examination of the worldview and basic values ingrained in Euro-western consciousness and Christian theological presuppositions is required, and a return to the question of the whole of theology. An evolutionary framework broadens the historical framework beyond biblical and even human history. A cosmological or evolutionary starting point has moved most ecotheologians to conclude that the primary religious story is that of the emergence of life: immanent, transcendent and panentheistic. This starting point offers a common creation story. Sallie McFague suggests that such a common creation story could become the beginning of an 'evolutionary, ecological, theological anthropology that could have immense significance transforming how we think about ourselves and our relations and responsibilities toward other human beings, other species, and our home, planet Earth' (McFague 1993: 33).

To genuinely take evolution seriously in light of the ecological crisis requires us to re-acquaint ourselves with the divine presence revealed within the natural world, and to revere the book of nature, as said the Celts. This is an ancient awareness within all cultures, and present at times within the Christian tradition in the works of Thomas Aquinas, Hildegaard of Bingen, Meister Eckhart and Pierre Teilhard de Chardin. To encounter the sacred in the natural world moves us to resist its destruction. To ponder that every leaf or snowflake from time immemorial is unique breaks opens our understanding of creativity beyond the imaginable. To give up humanity as the pinnacle of creation and superior life form allows one to see the magnificence of the universe, the complexity of life on earth and the radical dependence humans have upon the earth community. To ponder the story of the universe makes evident that religious consciousness arises from the universe processes itself. Humans are integral to, not dominant over, this amazing drama.

A cosmological approach is enormously challenging to religious understanding, and is profoundly divergent from stewardship. If we decide to start an ecotheological analysis with an evolutionary cosmology, then the history of the universe, the primary religious story, is the context in which we reflect upon the order of magnitude of this crisis. The universe is:

> [...] the primary sacred community, the primary revelation of the divine, the primary subject of incarnation, the primary unit of redemption, the primary referent in any discussion of reality or of value. Any human activity must be seen primarily as an activity of the universe and only secondarily an activity of the individual. (Berry 1985: 6)

The universe and the earth are seen as both spiritual and physical. Life is a community of beings where in each is an articulation of life's diversity as well as a mode of divine presence, and each functions in unique and critical ways for the health and creativity of the whole. Berry writes:

> ...the universe carries the deep mysteries of our existence within itself. We cannot discover ourselves without first discovering the universe, the earth and the imperatives of our own being. Each of us has a creative power and a vision far beyond any rational thought or cultural creation of which we are capable. Nor should we think of these as isolated from our own individual being or from the earth community. We have no existence except within the earth and within the universe. (Berry 1988: x)

Ecofeminism, Evolution and Cosmology

When ecofeminists address cosmology they add the analysis of gender. Examples will illustrate how ecofeminist theologians have taken cosmology and evolution to be their starting points. Ruether proposes an ecofeminist theocosmology using science and an organistic view of the universe. If Christianity were reoriented towards a cosmological horizon it may foster a renewed spirituality of earth. Such an ecological spirituality would awaken a sense of kinship and communion with the earth community, filling our spirits with compassion, and developing an 'I-Thou relationship' with all forms of life and with 'the great Thou, the personal centre of the universal process' (Ruether 1992: 251–2).

A cosmological framework provides both a common creation story, a liberatory cultural narrative from which to respond to the ecological crisis and a grounding from which to reinterpret theological convictions. If theology were to consider the earth to be the basic context of its reflection, this would suggest a common agenda for all theological endeavour, according to McFague. Briefly summarized, such a process would involve an ongoing deconstruction of the anthropocentrism and hierarchical dualisms that have permeated many of the theological depictions of reality, and cause to socio-ecological wreckage. McFague writes that this common earthly agenda would:

> [...] turn the eyes of theologians away from heaven and towards earth; or more accurately, it causes us to connect the starry heavens with the earth, as the common creation story claims. [...] In whatever ways we might reconstruct the symbols of God, human being, and earth, this can no longer be done in a dualistic fashion, for the heavens and the earth are one phenomenon, albeit an incredibly ancient, rich and varied one. (McFague 1993: 87)

Ivone Gebara is someone who has tackled systematic theology in depth from both an ecofeminist and cosmological framework. The evolutionary scope and the breath of inclusion from cosmology are connected to a concrete option for the marginalized, as described in her book *Longing for Running Water: Ecofeminism and Liberation* (1999). The task, she says, is urgent to challenge and change the Christian theological structures that are implicated in the interconnected destruction of the Earth's body, the human body and relationships to all living bodies. Gebara develops an ecofeminist epistemology to assist the immense task of reconstructing our cultural, cosmic and vital reference points (Gebara 1999: 23). She claims that the evolutionary creative processes need to be the foundations for theology, and reshape anthropology in intricate levels of relatedness and ecological interdependence. Gebara addresses theological God-talk by returning to religious experience as the basis of theology. The cherished notions of a pure and personal God, explicit revelation, resurrection and salvation are significantly altered and unequivocally relativized. A universal Christology is replaced with a just, kind, inclusive Jesus. Theology is to be more 'humble, existential, tentative and open to dialogue' (Gebara 1999: 54). In turn it will be more accountable to its social consequences, to truths as open-ended, to tentative understandings of existence, and to a letting go of absolute statements.

Anne Primavesi is yet another ecofeminist theologian who has entered deeply into the conversations between theology and science, based on the Gaia hypothesis as developed by James Lovelock (Lovelock 1982, 1990). The Gaia hypothesis supports an evolutionary and scientific understanding of the earth, and suggests that the earth functions like a whole organism. It is a whole life system, maintaining a sophisticated equilibrium barely perceptible to humans. When one delves deeply into evolutionary biology, ecology or geology the divisions between plant and animal, living and non-living, and spirit and matter begin to dissolve. These distinctions simply do not make sense from an earth sciences viewpoint. This knowledge is then brought to bear upon the Christian theological system, with its hierarchical dualisms and Christocentric claims. If science is the starting point for theological reflection, then religion must be understood quite differently.

Primavesi is one of the few ecofeminists who uses earth science in depth. Recognized for her ecofeminist critique of hierarchy, and its entrenchment in theology, her books *Sacred Gaia* (2000) and *Gaia's Gift* (2003) offer additional and extraordinary reflections on theology if it were to take evolution and the earth processes seriously. In this perspective theology becomes another earth science, meaning one that raises questions about the human status before God as we see ourselves within the context of relationships between organisms and their ecosystems that constitute the world. Similar to others Primavesi criticizes Christianity for only considering human history as relevant, and indeed only the stories and cultures of particular groups of people. Evolutionary science obliges us 'to study the world from whose history we are largely absent' (Primavesi 2000: 21). For example, the doctrine of human supremacy must be challenged. Being 'made in God's image' cannot apply only to humanity. As elsewhere, when these change other Christian beliefs are affected. Notions of revelation, redemption, incarnation and soteriology currently depend on an anthropocentric base.

When the theological base is changed to include the history and the whole of life, it is easy to see why ecofeminist theologians call for radical changes at the foundation of theology. One cannot help but be inspired by the expansiveness of life, and the genius and creativity of the emergence of life on earth. One's image of God enlarges to a breathtaking point. The incarnation is expanded and intensified to embrace the earth. Revelation becomes the sensing of a sacred presence revealed through all of life processes. The world/earth is much more awesome, extraordinary and sacred than previously appreciated!

These examples offer a glimpse at how ecofeminist theologians dialogue with the earth sciences. What is distinct about some ecofeminist analyses is their inclusion of justice with cosmology and evolution (Eaton 1998). They find a way to blend earth sciences or cosmology with issues of equity, justice, rights and life abundant. It is not sufficient to reinterpret theology within the history of the earth or the universe. Without an understanding of human systems of domination, in both their ideological and material forms, and the intricate connections between the domination of women and nature, a renewed earth theology may only offer an inspirational orientation.

Cosmology and Ecofeminist Justice
The deterioration of the earth is woven into social inequities to such a degree that ecojustice must be bonded to social justice. The growing numbers of poor people bear the direct and immediate cost of ecological ruin. Yet they are stripped of decision-making power as the transfer of regional resources going to larger institutions increases. The decision-makers are frequently inaccessible to local people and impervious to their needs. Further, many people are kept in a state of confusion by corporate media regarding the causes of their distresses. Those who resist are held hostage by layers of a system that is not accountable for the consequences of their actions – not to people, land, or animals – only to economic benefit. Feminist economist Marilyn Waring shows that most of life's work, women's work in particular and ecological disasters are not calculated into the economic costs or benefits (Waring 1988). Even social and ecological disasters such as the Gulf wars or the oil spill of the Exxon Valdez actually register as economic gains! When toxic substances are routinely dumped in Black or Hispanic neighbourhoods, when asthma is epidemic in children due to air pollution, when women have their land seized by corporations, when Northern elites require exotic coffees, and fresh flowers or mangoes in winter and poor Southern workers are forced to oblige, then we must talk of ecojustice in addition to earth sciences. One is insufficient without the other. Some ecofeminist theologians blend the two, with some emphasizing the earth sciences while others emphasize ecofeminist liberation theologies, and many do both.

Ecofeminist Liberation Theologies

Ecofeminist theologians articulate the need to develop a radically new way of doing theology in a coalescing of ecological, feminist, and liberationist theologies. The starting point for ecofeminist liberation theologies is the plight of the oppressed, in particular women and the natural world. Liberation theologies apply the axiom of Karl Marx, that is, the goal is to change the world, and not simply to reflect and interpret it.

Some examples of such work will show how ecofeminist liberation theologians are both reflecting theologically on particular circumstances, as well as trying 'to change the world'. As mentioned in Chapter One, it is impossible to track those who use ecofeminism in their work and daily lives. In addition to those who teach and write on ecofeminism, I know women for whom ecofeminist analysis is a factor in trying to stop road construction, prevent genetically modified foods, get pesticides off public lands, and preserve a wildlife sanctuary. I know that ecofeminist spiritualities inspire political activists working on housing, safe water, cancer research, agriculture and fisheries. Women use ecofeminist liberation views in film-making, art, rituals and writing. I also know women who work at home raising their children with a consciousness of the earth and gender issues. And there are many women and men who are not 'out there doing' but who orient their energies in quiet and subtle ways compatible with ecofeminism, although they have never heard the term.

It is time, as suggests Mary Grey, to hear from those acting and reflecting directly out of their own struggles, and not from those trying to include their voices (personal communication, 12 March 2001). In this vein here are four distinct examples of ecofeminist liberation theology, and which represent only a few who do this work.

The first is the work of Ekta Panishad, a Gandhian land reform organization in India.[4] Jill Carr Harris, a Canadian living for decades in India, facilitates land issues for women in Bihar, a very poor area of India. Land is the main resource and owning land confers social status. Few women own land and they suffer a low social status and personal insecurity. When caste is involved, those from upper castes prevent lower caste women who are Dalit or Untouchable from owning land. Harris's work, directly with the women, is to obtain land rights for women as part of a larger land distribution program. In Bihar women are very vulnerable because of a high degree of social violence. Women's groups found that one out of every five women is a victim of constant physical abuse. In strengthening women to preempt such violence, women need to be given greater status within the home. As land endows power and status, women's control over land resources is one method to

---

4.   Jill Carr Harris, *Women and Land Right* (Presented on Women and Land Rights Day, 7 October 2003; Patna, Bihar. Personal communication).

ensure lower levels of domestic violence. In Kerala, a study on the relation of domestic violence and land was carried out which showed that women without land suffer a fifty per cent greater incidence of domestic violence. Women with a house and property only experienced about eight per cent (Agarwal 1994).

There is resistance to women owning land that comes through complex patriarchal social ideologies and practices around marriage rights, dowry and familiar arrangements. In addition, men want exclusive control over farming operations. They plough the fields, and although women do twelve out of the routine fourteen farming operations they are not considered 'the farmers', in spite of it being well known that women's decisions in land management improve family well-being. The work of Ekta Panishad is to go from village to village, usually walking in a Gandhian method, to educate the women and men as to these issues, and to pressure the local and regional governments to change the laws. Harris's work on gender and land is motivated by a feminist analysis, a Christian social justice vision, Gandhian training in non-violence, and a respect for the complex relationship between women, livelihood, and relatedness to the land. This is one form of ecofeminist liberation theology.

A second example is about the desperate lives of women in Rajasthan. Eco-feminist theologian Mary Grey has, for years, travelled to Rajasthan as part of a project Wells for India. The goal is to get clean water, and also to mitigate the lethal combination of tradition, religion, caste, poverty and patriarchy that 'entrap the lives of women in unremitting drudgery' (Grey 2003: 28). Female infanticide, anaemia, poor nutrition, and maternal mortality are daily realities here. Rainfall in Rajasthan is unpredictable, and water projects funded by the World Bank and other schemes of economic globalization are causing serious health problems, water shortages and salination, and food deficits. The severity of the situation is extreme, and the need for theologians to take these dire realities seriously cannot be overstated. Reflecting on this work in Rajasthan, Grey brings the situation to theology and shapes an effectual ecofeminist liberation theology in *Sacred Longings: Ecofeminist Theology and Globalization* (2003). The need for a practical ecofeminist liberation theology to be transformative and meaningful to these kinds of situation is the conversation throughout the book. Grey finds resources in spiritualities of the desert, of water, in theologies of ethical restraint, liberation and flourishing, in biblical stories such as that of Miriam, and in ecomysticism. Working within the dialectics of the concrete realities of suffering, the need to alleviate the pain and confront the causes, and, to name theological strengths and obstacles are another form of the work of ecofeminist liberation theologies.

A third example is the story of Con-spirando, a Chilean-based women's collective working in the areas of ecofeminism, liberation theology and spirituality throughout Latin America. Founding member Judy Ress describes Con-spirando and develops an ecofeminist liberation theology in her book *Without a Vision the People Perish: Reflections on Latin American Ecofeminist Theology* (2003). Begun in 1991, Con-spirando is both a local group and part of a web of ever expanding networks to devise a viable and sophisticated global force.[5] Con-spirando began modestly among friends who came together for creative rituals and feminist reflections. Word spread and it grew. Each took turns to plan the rituals. They shared their stories, heartaches and joys through drama, dance, music and poetry; through earth, fire, water and wind; through native Mapuche or Aymara chants and drums; through silence; often through tears. The members of the Con-spirando collective agree that it was these rituals that brought them into being. Con-spirando is now a network with three characteristics: (1) a feminist perspective; (2) a spirituality and a theology adequate for women; (3) a commitment to the earth as both sacred and as source of life. Con-spirando's major achievements include: (1) the creation of a centre for feminist spirituality and theology that attracts people from all over the world; (2) the creation of a magazine where feminist and religious themes are debated; and (3) a link between the South and the North in terms of members, and exchanges of theologies, rituals, texts and resources. Con-spirando expresses, educates and develops yet another version of ecofeminist liberation theology.

A fourth example comes from the situation of fisherwomen in Newfoundland Canada. The current global trends of export-oriented fishery production and high technology stand in conflict with a subsistence and locally driven fishery. It spells disaster for the already strained ocean-ecosystem. In 1992 the federal government issued a moratorium on cod fishing; and cod was the chief livelihood of the fisheries. This crashed the economy and livelihood of Newfoundland's coast. Women in Newfoundland and Labrador are facing a time of crisis and decision-making in the largest ecological and cultural transition to impact Canadians in several decades, perhaps even in centuries. Prior to this, women working in the fishery were unrecognized, and their contributions to the fisheries were invisible. They had been excluded already from decision-making. As a result of the ending of fishing as a way of life, women have become immersed in a sense of personal and cultural re-evaluation. Women are looking to build redemptive pathways to sustainability. They know the sea

---

5.   The World Social Forum represents the coalescing of decades of social critical analysis and NGO work. Many theologians are involved in the World Social Forum.

has limits and an unjust death was imposed upon the ocean. Darlene Brewer of Newfoundland is studying their resilience of spirit and their struggle to make something livable of this crisis. She uses ecofeminist theological analyses to explore the contextual, lived experiences of these women. She sees in their lives the places of sin, hope, and wholeness. She reinterprets 'redemptive living', though fragmentary, within their sacred collective of life.

There are many more ecofeminist liberation efforts, such as Aruna Gnanadason supporting the struggle for life – water, land, living space – that permeates the lives of poor Indian women. Against the forces of death has evolved an eco-centred feminist spirituality of resistance within the concept of Shakti. Ivone Gebara works with women in the slums of Recife. Hyun Kyung brings the lives of Korean women to bear on her theological analyses. Gladys Parentelli of Venezuela celebrates the intrinsic love of life and children shared by poor women, and their shrewd ability to create and sustain life even amidst the most abhorrent conditions. Denise Ackermann and Tahira Joyner bring earth-healing in South Africa from both Christian and Muslim viewpoints, analysed within the legacy of domination and patriarchal apartheid that has scarred the country. These ecofeminist analyses are attending to the lived realities of women. Ecofeminist liberation theologies are developed by specific people in particular situations. It has many forms. What characterizes ecofeminist liberation theologies from other forms of theology is that they start from and return to concrete life realities, using a variety of tools to analyse both the causes of problems and viable solutions.

Ecofeminism Everywhere?

Is ecofeminism relevant everywhere? Some, who have studied ecofeminism for years and even developed ecofeminist analyses, have become aware of limitations when ecofeminism confronts particular cultural and concrete problems. Are connections between women and nature the same everywhere? Does ecofeminism make sense in the face of deforestation, drought, pollution, militarization and the socio-economic impoverishment of many of the world's women? In front of international corporate forces of globalization, does ecofeminism make any sense? Do Taiwanese Buddhist women see any potential in ecofeminist analyses? Ecofeminism as a meaningful cross-cultural analysis is spreading, but it is not uniform and does not take shape in the same way in each context.

In *Ecofeminism and Globalization*, the task was to see if ecofeminism actually makes sense in multiple contexts, cultures and religion (Eaton and Lorentzen 2003). The book looks at the intersection of ecofeminism and globalization from different cultural perspectives, and regions: Taiwan, Mexico, Kenya, Chile, India, Brazil, Canada, England and the United States. It includes voices from Hindi, Moslem, the indigenous Mijikenda from Kenya, and various Christian, Buddhist and Shinto traditions. The project had three goals: to create a conversation between ecofeminism and different aspects of globalization; to bring ecofeminism into greater awareness of the material realities and consequences of patriarchy; and to see if the ecofeminist claim of women/ nature constructs is cross-cultural and across religions. The conversations revealed that ecofeminism is effective in some contexts and not in others, with some religions and not with others. It was also evident that in confronting the multiple forces of globalization, ecofeminism is naive, uninformed and feeble.

Ecofeminism is an important and useful analysis. It is not, however, a global constant that can be simply applied. Patriarchal cultures are distinct in how the women/nature nexus is conceptualized and functions, and which religious aspects are used and for which purposes. A generic discourse about ecofeminism and religion breaks down when culture, context, religion and social norms are taken seriously.

Conclusion

From the cosmos to the city, from large horizons to particular contexts and cultures, and from a plurality of religious traditions, ecofeminism is valuable. The dialogue between cosmology and earth sciences is stretching ecofeminist theologies, in addition to the critiques of androcentrism and anthropocentrism, of liberation theologies, and of multi-religious realities. Ecofeminist theologies connect the cosmic with the social. This dance between a cosmic evolutionary horizon and a context/culture specific analysis is most challenging, and hazardous. At what point does the evolutionary framework overpower the specific context? How far can social and ecological ethics be deduced from evolutionary processes, given we know so little about them? While the cosmos is inspiring, the daily drudgery remains locked in complex systems of domination and ecosystems decline.

We need a cosmological theology that embraces a liberationist methodology and an eco-social justice perspective. While cosmology is concerned with broad horizons and worldviews, ecofeminism offers substantial analyses of the theoretical underpinnings, the systems of domination, and, the global manifestations promoting and sustaining the linked socio-ecological crises. In its essence, this ecofeminist cosmological perspective is deeply moral and it is predominantly oriented towards praxis (Rasmussen 1991). The two components, cosmology and concrete praxis that consolidate socio-political and ecological goals, can unite. Anne Clifford remarks: 'These two areas, cosmology and praxis, will likely provide the guiding questions for the expression of belief in God who is both source of and ground for the world we inhabit and our destiny and hope' (Clifford 1991: 246).

Chapter Five

At the Intersection of Ecofeminism and Religion: Directions for Consideration

What is the state of the question at the intersection of ecology, feminism and religion? How can we continue to cultivate insights and actions such that this intersection can bear more 'traffic', moving in advantageous directions? Chapter One presented the many routes to and from the ecofeminist intersection, how they developed and where they converge and diverge. The second chapter dealt with the women/nature nexus. It offered a a glimpse at the histories and theoretical reasons for the domination of women and the exploitation of the earth, and where they are interrelated. The third chapter began a reflection on ecofeminism and theology, discussing some of the methodological quagmires, and giving examples of the range of ecofeminist theological efforts. The fourth chapter brought into view two of the most significant ecofeminist theological streams; the dialogues with the earth sciences and ecofeminist liberation theologies.

As ecofeminism develops and seeps into religious awareness, several general hermeneutics are surfacing. Viewed as a whole, they can be helpful in strengthening the religious ecofeminist discourses in general, and in specific ways create connections among the various voices claiming an ecofeminist perspective. This chapter will collect these hermeneutics and reflect on their significance for ecofeminism and religious reflection. While religion needs to be taken seriously within the range of ecofeminist work, my emphasis is on what ecofeminist *religious* thinkers and activists need to take seriously. The guiding question is: What hermeneutics will assist in the development of adequate ecofeminist religious conversations that are sufficiently comprehensive to be of genuine transformative value? At times I refer to Christian theology and at other times to religion in general. These hermeneutics can be useful for both. I have gathered the eight most relevant hermeneutics that have guided this book and that may be of assistance. These are:

1. a recognition of the multi and interdisciplinary character, of the breadth and depth of ecofeminist analyses, and of the need to collaborate to gain new insights;

2. an in-depth awareness of the logic of domination; the interlocking patterns of oppressions and the critical theories of liberation informing ecofeminist theory(ies);

3. critical appraisals of the destructive and liberating elements within religious traditions, especially with respect to the oppressed and the earth;

4. an appreciation for the exchange between science and religion, and the need for religions, specifically Christianity, to take evolution seriously;

5. a rigorous understanding of the extent of the ecological crisis;

6. an openness to reinterpretations in light of the myriad religious traditions, and a willingness to be transformed by inter-religious dialogue;

7. a commitment to politically relevant and engaged work in tandem with an awareness of the strained material realities of many peoples, and the necessity of religious voices to be active within the political and governmental arenas;

8. a receptiveness to new spiritual insights and religious experiences.

In what follows I will discuss each of these hermeneutics, affirming the transformative potential of ecofeminist theologies, noting certain limitations, and proposing future directions. The main thrust is to orient ecofeminist religious work to larger horizons of reflection and critical analysis, with a specific view to forge strong links between theory and praxis in ecofeminist religious – predominantly Christian – discussions. The critical relationship between theory and practice is a central preoccupation of feminist and liberation theologies; that is a commitment to concrete changes in a situation that will contribute to liberation at all levels of experience (Hewitt 1995: 5). This requires a consciousness of the dynamic interplay between theory and praxis, and of the political and practical dimensions of theory. If ecofeminist religious theories hold transformative value, then these hermeneutics may offer directions for future development.

1. A recognition of the multi- and interdisciplinary character, of the breadth and depth of ecofeminist analyses, and of the need to collaborate to gain new insights
Although it is difficult to be fully aware of the breadth of ecofeminism, to speak of ecofeminist perspectives one needs to be aware of the variations encompassed by the term. Ecofeminism has many origins and is many things. Approaches, issues, methods and practices are pluralistic. Ecofeminism spans a wide genre of styles.

It is important to appreciate ecofeminism as an intersection of many realities and voices, hence the image of a traffic roundabout with many roads in and out. Other metaphors are that ecofeminism is an umbrella term, a lens, a set of analyses, a symbol for a change of consciousness, a vision, or an insight into alternative ways of understanding, organizing and relating to the world. One could say that ecofeminism is experienced, interpreted and appropriated in different ways depending upon the social situation and context. Ecofeminists reflecting from religious perspectives could improve their awareness of the general lines of development of ecofeminist theories and praxis. It can be easier to just take a fragment of the women/nature nexus and call it ecofeminism, without either being informed by the large spectrum of ecofeminism, or not adequately considering it. For example, a feminist colleague was publishing and teaching on ecofeminism and the Christian doctrine of creation, yet she knew little about the extent of ecofeminism and nothing about the actual doctrine of creation and its lack of concern for the earth.

There is also a tendency to mention connections between women and the earth, women and nature, and even their mutual oppressions without having the slightest idea of either the history or the current problems. To bring ecofeminism into dialogue with religion requires more than a passing comment and a minimal understanding of the research, analyses and critiques. Most ecofeminist analyses are developing outside of religious conversations. It is necessary to be in dialogue with the many voices using the term such that ecofeminist religious contributions are beneficial to others.

2. An in-depth awareness of the logic and practices of domination; the interlocking patterns of oppressions and the critical theories of liberation informing ecofeminist theory(ies)
Ecofeminists have reflected extensively on the theoretical substructures of the patterns of domination characteristic of Euro-western societies. They claim that all forms of dominations are interdependent through conceptual frameworks that then propagate ideological, social and material forms of domination. Oppression based on ethnicity, class, gender, sexual orientation, colonialism and ecological exploitation are mutually sustaining patterns.

A predominant issue for Christian ecotheology is the extreme anthro-pocentrism that has permeated not only the teachings but also the religious imagination and experiences. Ecofeminist theologians detect and critique both the andro- and anthropocentrism of the Christian traditions. However, do eco-feminist theologians attend sufficiently to the history and pervasive nature of domination? And although forms of dominations are inter-linked, not all domi-nation is about a women/nature nexus, and not all domination of women is related to the natural world, and vice versa.

Another difficulty about domination is that it is everywhere, and is at times subtle. 'Everyday violence is common rather than rare. It is the violence that is intertwined with, and therefore configures, people's everyday lives of public or private work, sustenance, recreation, and intimate relations' (Bar 1998: 45). The blatant, indirect and elusive forms of violence endured by women are a familiar feminist topic. There are feminist insights on why and how the every-day world is problematic, and how unexamined divisions exist between the 'everyday world' and the abstracted and academic reflection on this same world. The work of Canadian sociologist Dorothy Smith, carefully exposes how even radical liberation analysis can be disconnected from the everyday world. It can indirectly support what she calls 'the relations of the ruling apparatus' (Smith 1987).

Liberation theologies are one means of orienting theology to these complex issues of the world: one interpretation of Christianity that brings ethics to the core of theology. Critical theory is an ally to liberation theologies (Hewitt 1995). The starting point of critical theory is the oppression and suffering of a particular society, and it aims to expose the structures of relations causal to the distress. Critical theory can address the operations of knowledge in the delibera-tion of beliefs, activities, illusions and social constructions of the community. How do we use theory in ecofeminist theology, and what are the limits of theory? Theories are also seductive. It is easy to proclaim the grand, and seem-ingly utopic goals of ecofeminism and cease to attend to the material world. The theory/praxis dialectic is an essential preoccupation of feminist theories committed to concrete liberatory changes in the situation and lives of women (Hewitt 1995). Theories can become part of the strategy for change. Much of ecofeminism is activism: theory in motion.

However, the goal is not to reflect from an observational podium, but to enable ecofeminist theologies to be confrontational and transformative voices of resistance and vision, with insights into a viable and alternative future. The challenge to those connecting ecofeminism and religion is threefold: to be cognizant of the logic and issues of domination; to reflect within a liberationist methodology, and; to remain connected to the problematic of the everyday world.

3. Critical appraisals of the destructive and liberating elements within the religious traditions, especially with respect to the oppressed and the earth.
It is essential to be conscientious and candid about the negative legacies of religious heritages. Although it is too simplistic to capitulate to Lynn White's denunciation of Christianity, it is also naive to simply 'green' Christianity without coming to terms with the legacy of Christian cultures. Christianity shares complicity in predatory practices towards the natural world. It is, in part, this critical appraisal of the past that creates a necessary hermeneutic of suspicion about proposals made for the future. How is this best accomplished? Three options will be discussed.

First, there is a need to examine the effects of Christianity on cultures and their ecological integrity as it has traversed the world. Is there an ecological and feminist pattern to the inculturation of Christianity? How have the pre-existing ecological practices been absorbed? While some may say that the destructive forms of Christianity are an aberration of the religion, they are nonetheless real historical forms that profoundly influence the shape of relations.

The second is by way of Dorothee Sölle, who insists that we develop and clarify, 'again and again', the distinction between the oppressive and liberating elements of theology and religious traditions. We need to be mindful of the destructiveness that has resulted from religions. For example, she reminds us that the Christian doctrine of creation has had three oppressive consequences: (1) the total otherness of God and God's dominion over men, women, animals and the earth; (2) an idea of a godless, lifeless earth; and (3) human loneliness, presumed to be the *a priori*, incontrovertible essence of the human condition. She acknowledges that the ecological catastrophe has its roots, in part, in the Christian tradition. 'If we are to develop a new understanding of creation,' she writes, 'then we need a critical awareness of the destructiveness of our faith' (Sölle 1984: 20).

A third way to develop this critical appraisal is in dialogue with a sociology of knowledge: that is, that the type of social-political participation determines how the thinker formulates the problems, and hence limits solutions. In any attempt to address or redress the ecological crisis, it is imperative to acknowledge the socially situated roots of thought. We need to 'dig up the soil out of which the varying points of view emerge' (Mannheim 1936: 43), and to be aware of our eco-social location because this affects directly the approach to ecotheological issues (Rasmussen 1996). Within the proliferation of ecotheology publications there is often a lack of awareness of the relations between religious ideals, the political strata from which they emerge, to whom they speak, and the specific cultural context. It is important to think about what kind of knowledge religion is claiming. To claim that the earth is sacred is easy. To move people to experience and understand a sacred dimension to life, and be inspired to protect the earth community is not; it requires insights into the processes of knowing, or epistemology. According to Gebara, this is the first task of an ecofeminist theology; knowing how and what we know (Gebara 1999).

Only with the ability to assess the limits of a tradition and its detrimental impact can the strengths and insights be claimed. Then what is revelatory, insightful, and indeed wise will emerge. It is important to have some detachment from cherished beliefs in order to examine them from another vantage point. Ecofeminism provides such a vantage point.

4. *An appreciation for the exchange between science and religion, and the need for religions, and specifically Christianity, to take evolution seriously*

Several key ecofeminist theologians have written on the significance of the dialogue between science and religion, and the importance of an evolutionary horizon. This puts into relief the religious beliefs and assumptions about nature and what it means to be human. As mentioned, the prevailing Christian worldview is a profoundly human-centred ideology that continues to value the earth as a set of resources having no intrinsic value or sacred independence. Without a dialogue with science it is pointless to try to counter anthropocentric ethics. It is through the earth sciences that we learn an earth-centred ethics.

Earth sciences teach us about history, the immense history of the earth and its endless experiments and sequences that brought life forth. The earth teaches about interactive systems; the intricate climate and hydrologic cycles are enough to stagger the imagination for a lifetime! It took three billion years for the earth's life-support systems to stabilize the climate to make it hospitable for the astonishing complexity of life to emerge on this planet. Earth's climate system is delicately poised to be able to support an elaborate array of life forms that took millions of years of experimentation, refining, and balancing to arrive at mutually enhancing biosystems (Suzuki 1997). The earth's climate involves highly sophisticated systems of oxygen and carbon dioxide exchange. This includes a hydrologic cycle that moves molecules of water from salted oceans to clouds that release fresh rain water to be absorbed into the soil and taken up through plant cells into forest systems and released to be breathed by humans and transported by mosquitos to animals to fish to rivers and back to the ocean!

The earth teaches about abundance in the lushness and inconceivable diversity of life. The earth teaches about relationship; the infinite variety of relationships from the molecular to the planetary, and the unfathomable complex interdependent relationships within ecosystems, and among ecosystems, and the mystifying social relations among animals. To learn about the earth is to experience extravagant beauty, awesome vistas and chasms, intense drama, sublime elegance, grace, dignity and overwhelming wonder. The briefest of insights about the earth opens human experience, where we can effortlessly speak of religious themes, of wonder and awe, living silence, beauty, life-abundant, and goodness. To learn from science is to make possible a genuine rapport with the natural world.

To consider the earth and cosmology as a decisive framework is to know that religious consciousness is an emerging process within the larger evolutionary processes of the earth. To situate our religious traditions within the evolutionary processes of the earth allows us to see that human ideas about the world, and religious stories and traditions are a late development within the earth's story. To perceive the earth primarily as a whole, and humanity as an integrated element is no easy task for many Christians. To conceive of Christianity in light of an evolutionary cosmology calls for substantial re-evaluations and broadens the historical framework beyond religious and human history. As Grey writes, 'An ecofeminist theology of creation demands a radical re-thinking of all our cosmic, cultural and vital reference points' (Grey 2000: 486).

5. A rigorous understanding of the extent of the ecological crisis

It does not suffice to address a 'generic' ecological crisis, as is present in various ecotheology publications. To speak of a generic ecological crisis is to ignore the contextual specificities as well the range of issues involved. Ecofeminist Karen Warren, who has written extensively on the theoretical aspects, also argues for the need to be aware of the ecological crisis in specific terms such as water, forestry, soil erosion, agriculture and pollutants (Warren 1997: 3–20).

There are numerous resources available, from the annual *State of the World Report*, the GEO reports and innumerable accounts from the United Nations. Non-governmental organizations produce countless meticulous reports that give considerable data as to the evidence of the ecological crisis. Full awareness of the crisis will always be limited, but many ecotheology books contain little data about the ecological crisis. The familiar theological subjects are presented: scripture, Christology, sacraments, the church, etc. While these concerns are not negligible, one gets the impression is given that all that needs to happen is to change our thinking on religious tenets. For ecofeminist theology, it is insufficient to discuss only feminism or theology, as also happens at times, and to omit how it relates to an aspect of the ecological crisis. This weakens the analysis and the possibility of actual transformation

A different problem is the absence of ecological concerns in religion in general, feminist or otherwise. At the annual American Academy of Religion, a gathering of thousands of religious educators, less than one per cent of the topics deal with ecology. It is also not uncommon for entire faculties of theology or religious studies, while perhaps acknowledging the ecological crisis – even its centrality – to fail to address it professionally. There are those who add 'ecological issues' to a list of religious items, and there are still more who mention the ecological crisis in passing. However the tokenism trivializes the ecological crisis, and the status quo is maintained. Yet what could be more pertinent for the present and the future? To be aware of the specifics of the ecological crisis is one way to make connections that will stick.

To further the relationship between theology and the ecological crisis, continuity needs to occur between religious symbols, such as water, earth or air and the actual conditions of these elements. For example every week Christians proclaim or sing about the waters of life, baptismal waters, streams of running waters, and being refreshed, cleaned and purified by water. Yet the actual situation of water in many parts of the world is dire (de Villiers 1999). Weather patterns, desertification, irrigation, dams and aquifers are one set of problems. Pollution and toxins of all kinds saturating much of the earth's freshwater are a second. Scarcity, and the 'politics of water' emerging in China, United States, Canada, the Middle East and India, is a third. The proliferation of private, multinational companies obtaining water rights 'troubles the waters' even further. Theologically, it makes little sense to proclaim on the 'waters of life' when the problems surrounding water are acute and highly political. Thomas Berry writes, 'if water is polluted it can neither be drunk nor used for baptism. Both in its physical reality and its psychic symbolism it is a source not of life but of death' (Berry 1985: 4).

Another example of the need for ecological awareness is in the complex issues of biotechnology, considered here to be a subset of the larger ecological crisis.[1] Apart from a few, such as Celia Deane-Drummond, theologians are late getting on the scene. Yet, biotechnology is deeply embedded in the cultural projects and practices, and is part of the social, political and religious landscapes.

---

1. For an in-depth discussion of this material see the collection *Biotechnology and Genetic Engineering: Current Issues, Ethics and Theological Reflections*. See also Celia Deane-Drummond, *Theology and Biotechnology: Implications for a New Science* (1997).

There is a great need to map the 'real world' of biotechnology,[2] and to identify all the levels of reality in which biotechnology is structured and operative. From the major religious traditions there is no consensus on biotechnology issues (National Bioethics Advisory Group 1997). The religious leaders are scrambling to develop ethical paradigms equipped to address the current biotechnological ventures.

Apart from human cloning, biotechnology is rarely a religious issue. Cloning animals, disturbing genetic sequences in food staples, flounder genes in tomatoes, chicken genes in potatoes, firefly genes in corn, hamster genes into tobacco – the list in endless – are rarely considered. How can ecofeminist and other theologians proclaim the sacredness of the earth without delving deeply into the issues of biotechnology? Biotechnological intervention of intricate earth processes is accelerating at an alarming rate. Yet it is based on extreme ignorance and arrogance, and is the next phase of domination. Religions need to weigh in on ethics, the sacredness of life, and stand in reverence of the great 'biotechnology' of the earth-processes. Ecofeminist religious voices need to attend to the data of the ecological crisis as well as recover a sense of the mystery of the Divine in nature. A deep and nourishing sensitivity towards life engenders reverence, and this is a profound resource for religious awareness and activism.

6. An openness to reinterpretations in light of the myriad religious traditions, and a willingness to be transformed by inter-religious dialogue
The era of disparate and divided religious traditions needs to be over. While each religion has distinct contributions, collaboration is necessary for the world to face such a global and intertwined crisis. It is conceivable to begin to appreciate each religious tradition as offering specific insights and teachings within a tapestry of revelations (Berry 1988). We need to genuinely encounter the many religious perspectives and spiritual sensitivities, and be transformed by this process. It is urgent that the Christian tradition engage in non-partisan inter-religious dialogue, and reinterpret itself in light of the world's religions. The exclusive and semi-inclusive Christian attitudes often prevail in inter-religious efforts, and continue to support a supremacy of Christianity, albeit differently (Knitter 2002). This is a hindrance to finding political convergences among religions in the face of ecological concerns.

---

2.   I am borrowing this term from Ursula Franklin, *The Real World of Technology* (1990) taken initially from C.B. Macpherson, *The Real World of Democracy* (1998: 12).

The ecological crisis is giving rise to novel forms of inter-religious colla-boration. From local to international, with academics and religious leaders, in parishes and temples, using conferences and publications inter-religious synergy is increasing. This is a new face and form of inter-religious co-operation, and the emphasis is more on affecting public policy than on inter-religious ex-change. The world's religions are being summoned to address the spiritual and moral dimension of the ecological crisis. The World Watch Institute recog-nized religion as a significant force that could join with others to mitigate ecological ruin (State of the World Report 2003). Secular organizations are in-tegrating ecospirituality into their work, such as Greenpeace, the Sierra Club and the David Suzuki Foundation.

Inter-religious co-operation is changing in the face of the socio-ecological crisis, and three will be mentioned. The first is a shift in form, moving from the study of the histories, texts, doctrines, and worldviews to calling forth the spiritual resources of the world's religions to become a political force for an ecological sustainable future. There is an emerging alliance of religion and ecology, where resources are pooled rather than compared or analysed. An innovative initiative was launched at Harvard University that invited religious leaders and thinkers to engage their own traditions with the ecological crisis, acknowledge the problems, assess the resources and collaborate with others.[3] The second is content. Religious and ecological conversations are raising ques-tions about the nature of religious knowledge, and moving towards under-standing each religion as part of a tapestry of revelations. It requires, at times, a relativizing of specific truth claims in order to see a greater truth of the reli-gious dimension of human consciousness and societies. There is a resurgence of research into the nature of religion, both as a quest of the human spirit, and, as a spiritual base embedded within the processes of life itself. The third is a shift from dogma to ethics. Given the rapid rate of ecological destruction and the uncertainty of a sustainable future, substantial change in religious attitudes towards the natural world are imperative. The work of rethinking the relation-ship of humans to the earth, and the implications for economic patterns, equity and life-style, are urgent tasks. Drawing from the ethical core and codes of each tradition there are invaluable and necessary resources to include the natural world in ethical considerations.

3.   This ten volume series is published, with edited collections on each of the ten major world religions (Harvard University Press). Mary Evelyn Tucker and John Grim, with hosts of consultants from numerous disciplines, have created a Forum on Religion and Ecology to promote the conversation in educational settings, public policy, research and outreach. See Forum of Religion and Ecology (FORE), http://environment.harvard.edu/religion.

It is important to identify the transformative and prophetic insights and values of distinct traditions that will assist collaborative responses to the socio-ecological crises. This process involves critical understanding and empathetic appreciation of many traditions. It also requires creative reclaiming, revisioning and reconstructing of the resources and multi-layered symbol systems in world religions (Tucker 2003: 6–7). The central task, from an ecofeminist perspective, is to align religious efforts, and the spectrum of cosmologies, myths, symbols, rituals, values and ethical orientations, and self-understanding within the rhythms and limits of the natural world.

7. A commitment to politically relevant and engaged work in tandem with an awareness of the strained material realities of many peoples, and the necessity of religious voices to be active within the political and governmental arenas
There is a growing need for theologians and religious thinkers to be politically and socially-engaged. As Mahatma Gandhi is noted for saying, 'Those who think religion has nothing to do with politics, do not know the nature of religion.' A great proportion of Christian theology seems oblivious to the escalation of violence in the world, or of ecological stress, economic exploitation, misogyny and consumerism. I am reminded of the renowned comment of Dom Helder Camara.

> I dream of the day when the intellectual Catholic elite will place itself at the service of those in backward countries, studying the problems inherent in poverty and misery, in international justice and charity, and perhaps putting aside other projects, other theological topics which have had their day, which serve only for academic dissertations without any practical effect on the people.

Ecofeminist theology, while generally attending to the world, can also be less than ideal. There can be blind spots in Northern ecofeminism due to its emphasis on theory while not making concrete connections with the socio-economic system and ecological ruin that crushes the lives of so many women. It is important to 'recognize the ways in which the devastation of the earth is an integral part of an appropriation of the goods of the earth whereby a wealthy minority can enjoy strawberries in winter, while those who pick and pack the strawberries lack the money for bread and are dying from pesticide poisonings' (Ruether 1996: 5). Northern ecofeminism can fall prey to cultural escapism, illusions and irresponsibility with an excessive emphasis on theory and a failure to attend to the world. This renders ecofeminist theology not only powerless to face the real issues it is addressing, but worse still, can find itself indirectly participating in the destruction of the world while creating beautiful theories about alternative futures.

Ecofeminism is intended to be about praxis. This means active engagement with and resistance of the forces of destruction, and the promotion of alternatives. Ecofeminism means challenging power structures, resisting militarism, nuclear testing, genetic manipulations, unfair terms of trade, reductions to health, education and social programs, economic and ecological exploitation, and myriad other problems. Ecofeminist liberation theologies are better served when the socio-ecological crisis is central to the discourse, and the effectiveness of theories and activities are measured against the lived effects of these crises.

It is often easier to bring in ideas and cultural-symbolic notions about the women/nature nexus than the global political realities that mutually affect women and the natural world. Actual systems of domination are interwoven with ideas, social customs, daily practices and religious rituals. The stories from Rajasthan and Bihar demonstrate this readily. The more ecofeminist theologies are detached from cultural realities – from knowing the evidence and from the 'frail global networks of accountability' – the greater the chance will be that we are promoting liberal, albeit graceful, theologies with little or no political responsibility (Eaton 2000: 41–55; Keller, 1997: 56–66). Political discussions penetrate more profoundly into the existential foundation of thinking than those that addresses the various 'points of view' and examine only the theoretical relevance of an argument.

A further observation is that while ecofeminist critiques move into cultures, it is within small circles; well-educated women often working in or educated in Europe or North America. Who is ecofeminist theology, which has come predominantly from affluent cultures, trying to reach? From who does it come, who does it represent, and to whom does it speak? Globally, those engaged in ecofeminist works are of diverse ethnic origins. The spokeswomen may emerge from an educated social stratum, but often advocate for poorer women in grassroots movements.

In the political separations of North/South, affluent/impoverished, ruling and ruled classes ecological and feminist issues are not the same. In some places there is a genuine conflict between social justice and ecological sustainability. Certain countries are only just breaking free from the devastating effects of colonialization, and need economic supports. One way to do so is to join the economic globalization program of export markets: forests are logged, animals disappear, and land sold to agribusiness or for biotechnology experimentation. The cash influx is immediate, although not sustainable. The ecological conservation becomes the new elite agenda.

This is a terribly difficult and complex reality. When daily survival is threatened, ecological preservation is not the top priority. But to destroy biodiversity, to eradicate rainforests, to pollute the water, air, and soil, is to render conditions for life having any semblance of health impossible. It is when deliberations enter this realm of socio-ecological crises that the magnitude of the global predicament becomes stark. How will ecofeminist theology respond to this turbulent and suffering reality? How can we speak of survival of earth in front of massive human suffering? How can social justice and ecological health – not just sustainability, but the awareness of the abundance and magnificence of all life – be addressed together? Currently this is a great tension, at all levels, and from many agendas.

Given this context, how can ecofeminist religious efforts be knowledgeable of and in solidarity with those most marginalized? If it does not correspond in some way to the genuine realities, then it has little liberatory potential. If it does, then religions can be a social force, politically engaged, and ecologically transformative. Historically, deep spiritual movements are one of the most powerful forces to change the world.

8. A receptiveness to new spiritual insights and religious experiences

It is urgent for all religious traditions to reclaim their roots in the natural world. Each tradition has some awareness that the natural world is a primary place of revelation and religious experience. The beauty and elegance of the natural world have been inspirational and revelatory of the divine since time immemorial. It is only in recent history that this has not been so. In addition, the sentiments of awe and wonder are renowned as the basis of religious experience. It goes by many other names: reverence, contemplation, great mystery, mysticism and so on. Religions need to rediscover their roots in the world of awe and wonder, as both integral to religious experience and decisive at the nexus of religion, ecology and politics.

Awareness of the power of wonder and awe is available to anyone who spends time in the natural world. For instance, Daoism affirms:

> Those of us who contemplate the world soon come to have a great sense of wonder. The perfection of the stars, the beauty of mountains and streams, the invigorating quality of clean ocean air fills us with feelings of celebration and reverence. Reverence only comes with experience and care. We must be responsible, and at the same time express the wonder of all that we know as human.

Wonder and awe lead to reverence, and reverence leads to responsibility and ethics. Reverence for and responsibility to the natural world are intimately connected to each other, and to authentic religious experience.

Fostering a deep ecological awakening is a central role religions can play today. It is imperative that religious leaders reawaken an awareness of a sacred presence active within the earth's sublime and sophisticated life systems, to which the appropriate response is 'awe'. To see and know the earth as such requires a new way of perceiving, and a confidence that to experience a grove as sacred is not quaint, incidental, irrelevant, or even heretical. Religions need to reclaim their heritage, such that 'even the tiniest caterpillar is a book about God' (Meister Eckhart).

Ecologically oriented religious voices affirm that this kind of awareness is not a luxury, but the basis of religious experience and a necessary piece of ethical deliberations and political motivation. To consider life as sacred is termed superfluous, or romantic. It is legitimate to view life as a commodity and to discuss ecological ruin in credit and debit terms. Life is a market, not an intrinsic value. Yet this view is economically short-sighted, ecologically untenable, ethically reprehensible and religiously mistaken. The governing economic worldview needs to be countered with a more powerful and alluring understanding of life. The earth and its life forms are not a set of resources. Rather they are modes of divine presence. The difficulty is how to get from here to there!

The primary mode of knowing in Euro-western societies is analytic. Analysis sheds light on aspects of a situation, and can expose patterns, systems, causes and effects, and unmask power dynamics. It is the customary tool for feminists and ecofeminists. Yet analysis has its limits. Analysis cannot open the door to profound insights, to what can be known beyond all conventional knowing. Awe is a way of knowing, and provides a kind of data. It is a dimension of life-experience and the essence of religious awareness. Yet awe is often belittled, ignored or dismissed as irrelevant. It is accepted as a private experience, not a revelatory moment, as a personal spirituality not a crucial dimension of religious investigation. Still, awe is intimately bound to the essence of religion. Rabbi Heschel has observed:

> Awe is a sense for the transcendence, for the reference everywhere to the mystery in and beyond all things. It enables us to perceive in the world intimations of the divine. To sense the ultimate in the common and simple, to feel in the rush of the passing, the stillness of the eternal. What we cannot comprehend by analysis, we become aware of in awe. (Dresner 1997: 3)

The capacity for awe remains omnipresent: a quiet eminence that radiates everywhere. It creates an awareness of the extraordinary, abundant, unique and interconnected array of life. To marvel at the natural world within the large horizon of the cosmic adventure – and to understand that we are constitutionally embedded within this drama – requires a transcendence of our superficial worldviews and beliefs. Wonder and awe can become a way of seeing, of knowing, and of informing our political visions. Herein lies the terrain of genuine new insights, energies, understandings, ethics, analyses and awareness. From here can emerge a dynamic and consequential political energy and orientation.

Ecofeminism can bring this dimension into its intersection. The combination of the substantive analyses of the women/nature nexus, an in-depth awareness of domination, the inter-disciplinary interests and global reach, and the immense creativity are great assets within ecofeminism. To add an understanding of religious experience, and one that is embedded within the earth processes – without losing the social-political-ecological dimensions – would be very persuasive.

Nonetheless it remains that wonder and awe cannot be analysed; only experienced. As comments Rabbi Heschel, 'to become aware of the ineffable is to part company with words.' He writes:

> We can never sneer at the stars, mock the dawn or scoff at the totality of being. Sublime grandeur evokes unhesitating, unflinching awe. Away from the immense, cloistered in our own concepts, we may scorn and revile everything. But standing between earth and sky, we are silenced by the sight. (Dresner 1997: 2)

Conclusion

If, as Einstein says, problems cannot be solved at the level of consciousness in which they were created, then business as usual cannot continue. It is not simply that we need to rearrange our religious thinking and traditions. We need to understand the dialectic between religion and culture in order to make religion an active political player. In many parts of the world the religious right is very active politically. In fact, it is virtually the *only* religious voice that is sufficiently loud to be heard. This is not helpful, as their agenda, in North America at least, is pro-military, anti-environmental protection, anti-evolution, pro-family values (read women return to the patriarchal home), limited reproductive freedom, and little state intervention in business. This cannot continue. Other religious perspectives need to be in the arena. The ecological situation is dire, and the reality of many women's lives – endless restrictions, poverty, slavery conditions and early death – is immoral and contemptible. This is the ecofeminist challenge.

In this era of ecological, religious and political instabilities much is required of us. Ecofeminism is a fresh insight, and there are many roads to and from this insight. Ecofeminism offers a great deal of potential to understand and transform some of the exceedingly difficult problems of the era. It offers alternative options, new ideas, political possibilities, and renewed spiritualities.

New insights are emerging from evolution and inter-religious consciousness. Perhaps we can be inspired by the elegance and gracefulness of earth-life, imbued with the sacred presence that animates all life, and impelled to political action. Some questions persist, and speak to each of us. Poet Mary Oliver writes:

> Who made the world?
> Who made the swan and the black bear?
> Who made the grasshopper? This grasshopper, I mean –
> the one who is eating sugar out of my hand?
> Who is moving her jaws back and forth instead of up and down?
> I don't know exactly what prayer is.
> I do know how to pay attention,
> how to be idle and blessed, how to stroll through the fields
> Tell me, what else should I have done?
> Doesn't everything die at least, and too soon?
> Tell me, what is it you plan to do
> with your one wild and precious life?
> (Excerpts from The Summer Day)
>
> (Oliver: 94)

Bibliography

Adams, Carol J. (ed.)
    1990   *The Sexual Politics of Meat: A Feminist-Vegetarian Critical Theory* (New York: Continuum).
    1993   *Ecofeminism and the Sacred* (New York: Continuum)

Agarwal, Bina
    1992   'The Gender and Environment Debate: Lessons from India', *Feminist Studies* 18 (Spring): 119–58.

Alters, Brian and Sandra Alters
    2001   *Defending Evolution in the Classroom: A Guide to the Creation/Evolution Controversy* (Sudbury, MA: Jones and Bartlett, 2001).

Bal, Mieke
    1991   *On Story-Telling: Essays in Narratology* (ed. David Jobling; Sonoma, CA: Polebridge Press).

Bar On, Bat-Ami
    1998   'Everyday Violence and Ethico-Political Crisis', in Bat-Ami Bar On and Ann Ferguson (eds.), *Daring to be Good: Essays in Feminist Ethico-Politics* (New York: Routledge, 1998): 45–52.

Bateson, Gregory
    1972   *Steps to an Ecology of Mind* (New York: Ballantine Books).

Beavis, Mary Ann
    1991   'Stewardship, Planning, and Public Policy', *Plan Canada* 31.6 (November): 75-82.

Berry, Thomas
    1960–86   *Riverdale Papers*, Vols. 1-12 (New York: Riverdale Press).
    1988   *The Dream of the Earth* (San Francisco: Sierra Club Books).
    1999   *The Great Work: Our Way into the Future* (New York: Bell Tower).

Bertell, Rosalie
    1985   *No Immediate Danger? Prognosis for a Radioactive Earth* (Toronto: Women's Press).
    2001   *Planet Earth: The Latest Weapon of War* (Montreal: Black Rose Books).

Biehl, Janet
    1991   *Finding Our Way: Rethinking Ecofeminist Politics* (Montreal: Black Rose Books).

Birch, Charles, William Eakin and Jay B. McDaniel (eds.)
    1990   *Liberating Life: Contemporary Approaches to Ecological Theology* (Maryknoll, NY: Orbis Books).

Boff, Leonardo
    1995   *Ecology and Liberation: A New Paradigm* (Maryknoll, NY: Orbis Books).

Bradiotti, Rosi *et al.*
    1994   *Women, the Environment and Sustainable Development: Towards a Theoretical Synthesis* (London: Zed Books).

Bramwell, Anna
    1990   *Ecology in the 20th Century: A History* (New Haven: Yale University Press).

Capra, Fritjof
    1994   'Systems Theory and the New Paradigm', in Carolyn Merchant (ed.), *Ecology; Key Concepts in Critical Theory* (Atlantic Highlands, NJ: Humanities Press): 334–42.

Christ, Carol and Judith Plaskow (eds.)
    1979   *Womanspirit Rising: A Feminist Reader in Religion* (San Francisco: Harper and Row).
    1989   *Weaving the Visions: New Patterns in Feminist Spirituality* (San Francisco: Harper and Row).

Clifford, Anne
    1991   'Theology and Scientific Cosmology: The Task and the Challenge' (Paper delivered at the Catholic Society of America).
    1991   'Creation', *Systematic Theology*, 1 (ed. Frances Schüssler Fiorenza and John Galvin; Minneapolis: Fortress Press): 195–247.
    1992   'Feminist Perspectives on Science: Implications for an Ecological Theology of Creation', *Journal of Feminist Studies in Religion* 8: 65–92.

Cobb, John, Jr
    1990   'The Role of Theology of Nature in the Church', in Charles Birch, William Eakin, and Jay McDaniel (eds.), *Liberating Life: Contemporary Approaches to Ecological Theology* (Maryknoll, NY: Orbis Books): 261–72.

Collard, Andree and Joyce Contrucci (eds.)
    1988   *Rape of the Wild: Man's Violence against Animals and the Earth* (London: The Women's Press).

Conlon, James
    1990   *Geo-Justice: A Preferential Option for the Earth* (Winfield, BC: Woodlake Books).

Coontz, Stephanie and Peta Henderson (eds.)
    1986   *Women's Work, Men's Property: The Origins of Gender and Class* (London: Verso).

Daly, Mary
    1978   *Gyn/Ecology: The MetaPhysics of Radical Feminism* (Boston: Beacon Press).

Dankelman, Irene and Joan Davidson
    1988   *Women and Environment in the Third World: Alliance for the Future* (London: Earthscan Publications) 8.

Deane-Drummond, Celia E.
    1997   *Theology and Biotechnology: Implications for a New Science* (London: Geoffrey Chapman).
    2000   *Creation Through Wisdom: Theology and the New Biology* (Edinburgh: T&T Clark).

Diamond, Irene, and Gloria Feman Orenstein (eds.)
    1990   *Reweaving the World; The Emergence of Ecofeminism* (San Francisco: Sierra Club Books).

Doubiago, Sharon
    1990   'Mama Coyote Talks to the Boys', in Plant (ed.), *Healing the Wounds*: 40–42.

Dresner, Samuel (ed.)
    1997   *I Asked for Wonder: A Spiritual Anthology Abraham Joshua Heschel* (New York: Crossroad).

Dunn, Stephen and Anne Lonergan (eds.)
    1991   *Befriending the Earth: A Theology of Reconciliation Between Humans and the Earth: Thomas Berry and Thomas Clarke* (Mystic: Twenty-Third Publications).

Dyson, Martha
    1990   'Ecological Metaphors in Creation', *Daughters of Sarah* 16 (May/June): 24–27.

Eaton, Heather
    1996   'Ecological-Feminist Theology: Contributions and Challenges', in Dieter Hessel (ed.), *Theology for Earth Community: A Field Guide* (Maryknoll, NY: Orbis Books): 77–92.
    1998   'The Edge of the Sea: The Colonization of Ecofeminist Religious Perspectives', *Critical Review of Books in Religion* 11 (1998): 57–82.
    2000   'Ecofeminist Contributions to an Ecojustice Hermeneutic', in Norman Habel (ed.), *Earth Bible* (London: Sheffield Press): 54–72.
    2001   'Ecofeminism and Globalization', *Journal for Feminist Theology* (May): 41–55.

Eaton, Heather and Lois Lorentzen (eds.)
    2003   *Ecofeminism and Globalization* (Lanham, MD: Rowman and Littlefield Publishers).

D'Eaubonne, Françoise
    1974   *Le Féminisme ou la Mort* (Paris: Pierre Horay).
    1994   'Le Temps de L'Ecoféminisme', in Carolyn Merchant (ed.), *Ecology: Key Concepts in Critical Theory* (trans. Ruth Hottell; Atlantic Highlands, NJ: Humanities Press): 174–97.

Einstein, Albert
    1989   'Ideas and Opinions'. Quoted in John Polkinghorne, *Science and Creation: The Search for Understanding* (Boston: Shambhala, 1989): 97.

Eisler, Riane
    1987   *The Chalice and the Blade: Our History, Our Future* (San Francisco: Harper and Row).

Eller, Cynthia
    2000   *The Myth of Matriarchal Prehistory: Why an Invented Past Won't Give Women a Future* (Boston: Beacon).

Franklin, Ursula
    1990   *The Real World of Technology* (Montreal; Toronto: CBC Enterprises).

Fox, Matthew
    1983   *Original Blessing: A Primer in Creation Spirituality Presented in Four Paths, Twenty-Six Themes, and Two Questions* (Santa Fe, MN: Bear).
    1991   *Creation Spirituality: Liberating Gifts for the Peoples of the Earth* (San Francisco: HarperSanFrancisco).

Gardner, Gary T., *et al.*
    2003   *State of the World 2003: A Worldwatch Institute Report on Progress Toward a Sustainable Society* (New York: London; W.W. Norton).

Gebara, Ivone
    1999   *Longing for Running Water: Ecofeminism and Liberation* (Minneapolis: Fortress Press).

Gimbutas, Marija
    1991   *The Civilization of the Goddess: The World of Old Europe* (ed. Joan Marler; New York: HarperSanFrancisco).

Gnanadason, Aruna
    1994   'Women, Economy and Ecology', in David Hallman (ed.), *Ecotheology* (Maryknoll, NY: Orbis Books): 179–85.

Gray, Elizabeth Dodson
    1979   *Green Paradise Lost* (Wellesley, MA: Roundtable Press).
    1984   *Patriarchy as a Conceptual Trap* (Wellesley, MA: Roundtable Press).

Green, Elizabeth and Mary Grey
    1994   *Ecofeminism and Theology* (Kampen: Kok Pharos; Mainz: Matthias-Grünewald-Verlag).

Grey, Mary
    2003   *Sacred Longings: Ecofeminist Theology and Globalisation* (London: SCM Press).

Griffin, David Ray (ed.)
    1988   *The Re-enchantment of Science: Postmodern Proposals* (New York: State University of New York Press).

Griffin, Susan
    1978   *Women and Nature: The Roaring Inside Her* (New York: Harper & Row).

Hall, Douglas
    1990   *The Steward: A Biblical Symbol Come of Age* (Grand Rapids, MI: Eerdmans).

Hallman, David (ed.)
    1993   *Ecotheology: Voices from South and North* (Maryknoll, NY: Orbis Books).

Haraway, Donna
    1991   *Simians, Cyborgs, and Women: The Reinvention of Nature* (New York: Routledge).

Harris, Jill Carr
    2003   *Women and Land Rights* (Presented on Women and Land Rights Day, 7 October 2003; Patna, Bihar. Personal communication).

Harrison, Beverly Wildung
    1985   *Making the Connections: Essays in Feminist Social Ethics* (ed. Carol S. Robb; Boston: Beacon Press).

Haught John F.
    1984   *The Cosmic Adventure: Science, Religion and the Quest for Purpose* (New York: Paulist Press).
    1993   *The Promise of Nature: Ecology and Cosmic Purpose* (New York: Paulist Press).
    1999   *God After Darwin: A Theology of Evolution* (Boulder: Westview).

Herlihy, David
    1997   *The Black Death and the Transformation of the West* (ed. and intro. Samuel K. Cohn, Jr; Cambridge, MA: Harvard University Press).

Hessel, Dieter (ed.)
    1992   *After Nature's Revolt: Eco-Justice and Theology* (Minneapolis: Fortress Press).

Hewitt, Marsha
    1995   *Critical Theory of Religion: A Feminist Appraisal* (Minneapolis: Fortress Press).

Hinsdale, Mary Ann
    1990   'Some Implications of Ecofeminism for Christian Anthropology and Spirituality' (Paper delivered at the College Theology Teaching Workshop, New Orleans).

1991   'Ecology, Feminism, Theology', *Word and World* XI.2 (Spring): 156–64.

Hull, Fritz (ed.)

1993   *Earth and Spirit: The Spiritual Dimensions of the Environmental Crisis* (New York: Continuum).

Jantzen, Grace

1984   *God's World, God's Body* (Philadelphia: The Westminster Press).

Johnson, Elizabeth A.

1992   *She Who Is: The Mystery of God in Feminist Theological Discourse* (New York: Crossroad).

1993   *Women, Earth, and Creator Spirit* (New York: Paulist Press).

Keller, Catherine

1990   'Women Against Wasting the World: Notes on Eschatology and Ecology', in Diamond and Orenstein (eds.) 1990: 249–63.

1993   'Talking About the Weather: The Greening of Eschatology', in Carol Adams (ed.), *Ecofeminism and the Sacred* (New York: Continuum): 30–49.

Kheel, Marti

1991   'Ecofeminism and Deep Ecology: Reflections on Identity and Difference', *The Trumpeter* 8 (Spring): 62–72.

King, Ynestra

1990   'Healing the Wounds in the Nature/Culture Dualisms', in Diamond and Orenstein (eds.) 1990.

Knitter, Paul F.

2002   *Introducing Theologies of Religions* (Maryknoll, NY: Orbis Books).

Kyung, Chung Hyun

1994   'Ecology, Feminism and African and Asian Spirituality: Towards a Spirituality of Eco-Feminism', in David Hallman (ed.), *Ecotheology* (Maryknoll, NY: Orbis Books): 175–78.

LaChance, Albert and John Carroll (eds.)

1994   *Embracing Earth: Catholic Approaches to Ecology* (Maryknoll, NY: Orbis Books).

Lahar, Stephanie

1991   'Ecofeminist Theory and Grassroots Politics', *Hypatia: A Journal of Feminist Philosophy* 6 (Spring): 28–45.

Lerner, Gerda

1986   *The Creation of Patriarchy* (Oxford: Oxford University Press).

Livingston, John

1994   *Rogue Primate* (Toronto: Key Porter).

Lovelock, James

1990   *The Ages of Gaia: A Biography of Our Living Planet* (repr.; New York: Bantam [New York: Norton, 1988]).

1982   *Gaia: A New Look at Life on Earth* (Oxford: Oxford University Press).

Macpherson, C.B.

1998   *The Real World of Democracy* (Toronto: House of Anansi Press).

Macy, Joanna

1991   *World as Lover, World as Self* (Berkeley: Parallax Press).

Malone, Mary T.

2003   *Women and Christianity: From the Reformation to the 21st Century* (Ottawa: Novalis).

2002   *Women and Christianity: From 1000 to the Reformation* (Ottawa: Novalis).

2001   *Women and Christianity: The First Thousand Years* (Ottawa: Novalis).

Mangum, John (ed.)
1989   *New Faith-Science Debate: Probing Cosmology, Technology and Theology* (Minneapolis: Fortress Press).

Mannheim, Karl
1936   *Ideology and Utopia: An Introduction to the Sociology of Knowledge* (With a preface by Louis Wirth; translated from the German by Louis Wirth and Edward Shils; New York: Harcourt, Brace).

Matthews, Clifford and Roy Abraham Varghese (eds.)
1995   *Cosmic Beginnings and Human Ends* (Chicago: Open Court).

McDaniel, Jay
1995   *With Roots and Wings: Christianity in an Age of Ecology and Dialogue* (Maryknoll, NY: Orbis Books).

McFague, Sally
1993   *The Body of God: An Ecological Theology* (Minneapolis: Fortress Press).

McFarland Taylor, Sarah
forthcoming   *Green Sisters: Catholic Nuns Answering the Call of the Earth* (Cambridge, MA: Harvard University Press).

Mellor, Mary
1992   *Breaking the Boundaries: Towards a Feminist Green Socialism* (London: Virago Press).

Merchant, Carolyn
1982   *The Death of Nature: Women, Ecology and the Scientific Revolution* (New York: Harper and Row).
1992   *Radical Ecology: The Search for a Livable World* (New York: Routledge).

Mies, Maria
1986   *Patriarchy and Accumulation on a World Scale: Women in the International Division of Labour* (London: Zed Books).

Mies, Maria and Vandana Shiva
1993   *Ecofeminism* (London: Zed Books).

Milne, Patricia
1995   'No Promised Land: Rejecting the Authority of the Bible', in Phyllis Trible *et al.* (ed.), *Feminist Approaches to the Bible* (Washington: Biblical Archaeological Society): 47–73.

Moltmann, Jürgen
1985   *God in Creation: A New Theology of Creation and the Spirit of God* (San Francisco: Harper and Row).

Moore, James
1993   'Cosmology and Theology: the Re-Emergence of Patriarchy' (Paper presented at annual meeting of the American Academy of Religion, Theology and Science Group, Washington, D.C., Nov. 1993).

Nash, James
1991   *Loving Nature: Ecological Integrity and Christian Responsibility* (Nashville: Abingdon Press).

Neu, Diann L.
2002   *Return Blessings: Ecofeminist Liturgies Renewing the Earth* (Cleveland: Pilgrim Press).

Oelschlaeger, Max (ed.)
> 1995   *Postmodern Environmental Ethics* (Albany: State of New York Press).

O'Faolain, Julia, and Lauro Martines (eds.)
> 1973   *Not in God's Image: Women in History from the Greeks to the Victorians* (New York: Harper and Row).

Oliver, Mary
> 1992   *New and Selected Poems* (Boston: Beacon Press).

Pearson, Clive
> 2002   'On Being Public about Ecotheology', *Ecotheology* 6.

Ted Peters (ed.)
> 1989   *Cosmos as Creation: Theology and Science in Consonance* (Nashville: Abingdon Press, 1989).

Philipose, Pamela
> 1989   'Women Act: Women and Environmental Protection in India', in Judith Plant (ed.), *Healing the Wounds: The Promise of Ecofeminism* (Toronto: Between the Lines): 67–75.

Plant, Judith (ed.)
> 1989   *Healing the Wounds: The Promise of Ecofeminism* (Toronto: Between the Lines).

Plumwood, Val
> 1992   'The Atavism of Flighty Females', review of *Finding Our Way*, by Janet Biehl, in *The Ecologists* 22 (January/February): 36.
> 1993   *Feminism and the Mastery of Nature* (London: Routledge).
> 1995   'Androcentrism and Anthropocentrism: Parallels and Politics' (unpublished paper; The Twenty-Second Annual Richard Baker Philosophy Colloquium on Ecofeminist Perspectives, University of Dayton, OH, 30 March 1995): 12–13.
> 1994   'The Ecopolitics of Debate and the Politics of Nature', *Ecological Feminism*, ed. Warren: 64–87.

Ponting, Clive
> 1991   *A Green History of the World* (London: Sinclair-Stevenson, 1991).

Prentice, Susan
> 1988   'Taking Sides: What's Wrong with Eco-Feminism', *Women and Environments* (Spring): 9–10.

Primavesi, Anne
> 1991   *From Apocalypse to Genesis: Ecology, Feminism and Christianity* (Minneapolis: Fortress Press).
> 2000   *Sacred Gaia: Theology as Earth Science* (London: Routledge).
> 2003   *Gaia's Gift: Earth, Ourselves, and God after Copernicus* (London; New York: Routledge).

Pui-lan, Kwok
> 1995   *Discovering the Bible in the Non-Biblical World* (Maryknoll, NY: Orbis Books).

Rasmussen, Larry
> 1993   'Cosmology and Ethics', in Mary Evelyn Tucker and John Grim (eds.), *Worldviews and Ecology* (Lewisburg: Bucknell University Press): 173–80.
> 1996   *Earth Community Earth Ethics* (Maryknoll, NY: Orbis Books).
> 2001   *Worldviews* 5 (Special Issue on Thomas Berry).

Radford Ruether, Rosemary
> 1973   *New Woman/New Earth: Sexist Ideologies and Human Liberation* (New York: Seabury Press).

1983   *Sexism and God-Talk: Toward a Feminist Theology* (Boston: Beacon Press).

1991   'Ecofeminism: Symbolic Connections Between the Oppression of Women and the Domination of Nature' (Loy H. Witherspoon Lecture in Religious Studies; University of North Carolina, 31 October 1991): 1–17.

1992   *Gaia and God: An Ecofeminist Theology of Earth Healing* (San Francisco: Harper).

1993   'Ecofeminism: Symbolic Connections Between the Oppression of Women and the Domination of Nature', *Ecofeminism and the Sacred*, ed. Carol Adams, [[pages]] (New York: Continuum).

Radford Ruether, Rosemary (ed.)

1996   *Women Healing Earth: Third World Women on Ecology, Feminism and Religion* (Maryknoll, NY: Orbis Books).

Rae, Eleanor

1994   *Women, the Earth, the Divine* (Maryknoll, NY: Orbis Books).

Ress, Mary Judith

1993   'Cosmic Theology: Ecofeminism and Panentheism. An Interview with Brazil Feminist Ivone Gebara', *Creation Spirituality* (Nov/Dec): 9–13.

2003   *Without a Vision, the People Perish: Reflections on Latin American Ecofeminist Theology* (Santiago, Chile: Sociedad Con-spirando, Ltda.).

Roach, Catherine

2002   *Mother/Nature: Popular Culture and Environmental Ethics* (Indiana: Indiana University Press).

Robb, Carol S. and Carl J. Casebolt

1991   *Covenant for a New Creation: Ethics, Religion, and Public Policy* (Maryknoll, NY: Orbis Books).

Roberts, Alexander and James Donaldson (eds.)

1867–83   *Ante-Nicene Christian Library: Translations of the Writings of the Fathers Down to A.D. 325* (Edinburgh: T&T Clark).

Rogers, Raymond

1994   *Nature and the Crisis of Modernity: A Critique of Contemporary Discourse on Managing the Earth* (Montreal: Black Rose Books).

Sahtouris, Elisabeth

1989   *Gaia: The Human Journey from Chaos to Cosmos* (New York: Pocket Books).

2000   *Earth Dance: Living Systems In Evolution* (Lincoln, NE: University Press).

Sandilands, Catriona

1989   *Gaia: The Human Journey from Chaos to Cosmos* (New York: Pocket Books).

1999   *The Good-Natured Feminist: Ecofeminism and the Quest for Democracy* (Minneapolis: University of Minnesota Press).

Santmire, H. Paul

1985   *The Travail of Nature: The Ambiguous Ecological Promise of Christian Theology* (Philadelphia and Minneapolis: Fortress Press).

Seager, Joni

1992   'The Atavism of Flighty Females', review of Finding Our Way, by Janet Biehl, in *The Ecologists* 22 (Jan/Feb): 36.

1993   *Earth Follies: Coming to Feminist Terms with the Global Environmental Crisis* (New York: Routledge).

Shiva, Vandana

1988   *Staying Alive: Women Ecology and Development* (London: Zed Books).

Smith, Dorothy E.
    1987   *The Everyday World as Problematic: A Feminist Sociology* (Toronto: University of Toronto Press).

Sölle, Dorothee and Shirley A. Cloyes
    1984   *To Work and to Love: A Theology of Creation* (Philadelphia: Fortress Press).

Spretnak, Charlene
    1990   'Ecofeminism: Our Roots and Our Flowering', in Diamond and Orenstein (eds.): 8-9.

    1991   *States of Grace: The Recovery of Meaning in the Postmodern Age* (San Francisco: Harper).

Starhawk
    1989   *The Spiral Dance: A Rebirth of the Ancient Religion of the Great Goddess* (New York: Harper & Row [1979]).

    1989   'Feminist, Earth-based Spirituality and Ecofeminism', in Judith Plant (ed.), *Healing the Wounds: The Promise of Ecofeminism* (Toronto: Between the Lines): 174–85.

Steingraber, Sandra
    1997   *Living Downstream: An Ecologist Looks at Cancer and the Environment* (Reading, MA: Addison-Wesley Publishing).

Stone, Merlin
    1978   *When God Was a Woman* (New York: Harcourt Brace Jovanovich).

Sturgeon, Noël
    1997   *Ecofeminist Natures: Race, Gender, Feminist Theory, and Political Action* (London; New York: Routledge)

Suzuki, David with Amanda McConnell
    1997   *The Sacred Balance: Rediscovering our Place in Nature* (Vancouver: Greystone Books).

Sylvan, Richard and David Bennett
    1994   *The Greening of Ethics* (Cambridge, UK: White Horse Press; Tucon, AZ: University of Arizona Press).

Tilley, Terrence
    1995   *Postmodern Theologies: The Challenge of Religious Diversity* (Maryknoll, NY: Orbis Books).

Toulmin, Stephen
    1990   *Cosmolis: The Hidden Agenda of Modernity* (Chicago: Chicago University Press).

Toynbee, Arnold
    1974   *Toynbee on Toynbee: A Conversation Between Arnold J. Toynbee and G.R. Urban* (New York: Oxford University Press).

Tucker, Mary Evelyn and John A. Grim (eds.)
    1993   *Worldviews and Ecology* (Lewisburg, PA: Bucknell University Press).

Tucker, Mary Evelyn
    2003   *Worldly Wonder: Religions Enter their Ecological Phase* (with a commentary by Judith A. Berling; Chicago: Open Court).

De Villiers, Marq.
    1999   *Water Wars: Is the World's Water Running Out?* (London: Weidenfeld and Nicolson).

Waring, Marilyn
    1988   *If Women Counted: A New Feminist Economics* (intro. Gloria Steinem; San Francisco: Harper and Row).

Warren, Karen
    1987   'Feminism and Ecology: Making Connections', *Environmental Ethics* 9 (Spring): 3-19.
    1988   'Toward an Ecofeminist Ethic', *Studies in the Humanities* 15: 140–56.
    1990   'The Power and the Promise of Ecological Feminism', *Environmental Ethics* 12 (Summer): 125–46.

Warren, Karen (ed.)
    1991   'The Quilt of Ecological Feminism', *Woman of Power* 20 (Spring 1991): 64–68.
    1991   *Hypatia: Special Issue on Ecological Feminism* 6 (Spring).
    1994   *Ecological-Feminism* (New York: Routledge).
    1996   *Ecofeminist Philosophies* (Bloomington: Indiana University Press).
    1997   *Ecofeminism: Women, Culture, Nature* (Bloomington: Indiana University Press).
    2000   *Ecofeminist Philosophy: a Western Perspective on What It Is and Why It Matters* (Lanham, MD: Rowman and Littlefield).

Watts, Alan
    1958   *Nature, Man, and Woman* (New York: Pantheon).

White, Lynn, Jr
    1967   'The Historical Roots of our Ecologic Crisis', *Science* 155 (1967): 1203–207.

Wilson, W. (trans.)
    1867   The Writings of Clement of Alexandria in A. Roberts and J. Donaldson (eds.), *Ante-Nicene Christian Library* (Edinburgh), IV: 209.
    1991   *Women's Environment and Development Organization, Women's Action Agenda '21* (Miami: World Women's Congress Secretariat, World Women's Congress for a Healthy Planet, November).

Zayac, Sharon Therese
    2003   *Earth Spirituality: In the Catholic and Dominican Traditions* (Boerne, TX: Sor Juana Press).

Index of Authors

Other books in the
Introductions in Feminist Theology series

Introducing African Women's Theology
Mercy Amba Oduyoye

Mercy Amba Oduyoye describes the context and methodology of Christian theology by Africans in the past two decades, offering brief descriptions and sample treatments of theological issues such as creation, Christology, ecclesiology, and eschatology. The daily spiritual life of African Christian women is evident as the reader is led to the sources of African women's Christian theology. This book reflects how African culture and its multi-religious context has influenced women's selection of theological issues.
ISBN 1-84127-143-8
Paper, 136 pages
£14.99

Introducing Asian Feminist Theology
Kwok Pui-Lan

The book introduces the history, critical issues, and direction of feminist theology as a grass-roots movement in Asia. Kwok Pui-Lan takes care to highlight the diversity of this broad movement, noting that not all women theologians in Asia embrace feminism. Amid a diverse range of sociopolitical, religiocultural, postcultural, and postcolonial contexts, this book lifts up the diversity of voices and ways of doing feminist theology while attending to women's experiences, how the bible is interpreted, and the ways that Asian religious traditions are appropriated. It searches out a passionate, life-affirming spirituality through feminine images of God, new metaphors for Christ, and a reformulation of sin and redemption.
ISBN 1-84127-066-0
Paper, 136 pages
£14.99

Introducing Body Theology
Lisa Isherwood and Elizabeth Stuart

Because Christianity asserts that God was incarnated in human form, one might expect that its theologies would be body affirming. Yet for women (and indeed for gay men) the body has been the site for oppression. *Introducing Body Theology* offers a body-centred theology that discusses cosmology, ecology, ethics, immortality, and sexuality, in a concise introduction that proposes and encourages a positive theology of the body.
ISBN 1-85075-995-2
Paper, 168 pages
£16.99

Introducing a Practical Feminist Theology of Worship
Janet Wootton

Only three great women-songs are retained in the Bible: Deborah's song for ordinary people, Hannah's song of triumph, and Mary's song at meeting her cousin Elizabeth. Many others, such as Miriam's song, are truncated or overshadowed by male triumphs. *Introducing a Practical Feminist Theology of Worship* begins by revealing how women have been 'whispering liturgy.' It then explores female images of God, discusses how worship spaces function, and offers practical suggestions for how women can use words and movements to construct authentic forms of worship.
ISBN 1-84127-067-9
Paper, 148 pages
£14.99

Introducing Redemption in Christian Feminism
Rosemary R. Ruether

Introducing Redemption in Christian Feminism explores the dichotomy between two patterns of thinking found in Christianity: the redemption of Christ being applied to all without regard to gender, and the exclusion of women from leadership because women were created subordinate to men and because women were more culpable for sin. After examining these two patterns, Ruether addresses some key theological themes: Christology, the self, the cross, and eschatology.
ISBN 1-85075-888-3
Paper, 136 pages
£16.99

Introducing Thealogy: Discourse on the Goddess
Melissa Raphael

Introducing Thealogy provides an accessible but critical introduction to the relationship between religion, theo/alogy, and gender, especially as these concepts unfold in the revival of Goddess religion among feminists in Europe, North America and Australasia. Raphael focuses on the boundaries of that broad movement, what is meant by the Goddess, theology in history and ethics, the political implications of the movement, and how it relates to feminist witchcraft.
ISBN 1-85075-975-8
Paper, 184 pages
£19.99

Introducing Feminist Christologies
Lisa Isherwood

In this imaginative book, Lisa Isherwood challenges the oppressive model of an all-powerful God and highlights feminist interpretations of Christ across the globe. She attempts to chart a course from questioning the relevance of a male saviour to women – to the many faces of Christ that have emerged from the lives of women (Jesus as lover, friend or shaman, amongst other things) – to a place of reflection about the nature of Christological thinking in the twenty-first century.

ISBN 1-84127-250-7
Paper, 144 pages
£14.99

6526

DATE DUE

#47-0108 Peel Off Pressure Sensitive